Rescuing Patty Hearst

*M*emories from a Decade Gone Mad

Virginia Holman

Simon & Schuster

New York   London   Toronto   Sydney   Singapore

SIMON & SCHUSTER
Rockefeller Center
1230 Avenue of the Americas
New York, NY 10020

Copyright © 2003 by Virginia Holman

All rights reserved, including the right of reproduction in whole or in part in any form.

Simon & Schuster and colophon are registered trademarks of Simon & Schuster, Inc.

Designed by Jeanette Olender
Manufactured in the United States of America

10   9   8   7   6   5   4   3   2   1

Library of Congress Cataloging-in-Publication Data

ISBN 0-7432-2285-7

For information regarding special discounts for bulk purchases, please contact Simon & Schuster Special Sales at 1-800-456-6798 or business@simonandschuster.com

This book is for my sister and my father, who endured so much and who graciously submitted to numerous interviews and gave their total support to this project.

This book is also for my mother, whose losses are unspeakable.

I never could have written this book without the unstinting love and support of my husband and son. I'm all yours now, boys.

This is a work of creative nonfiction, of memory, of a world as I knew it. Venturing into the past is like taking a shot over the shoulder and the landscape of memory is, at best, viewed through a small and blighted mirror. The Names of people and places and certain characteristics have been changed. Specific dialogue, of course, has been recreated in keeping with my recollection of events.

I don't know what happened. I am just telling you what everybody thinks happened, what might have happened, what you are saying happened. If that is history, then I am telling you history.

—Rose Mary Woods, 1973

Life ain't nothin' but a funny, funny riddle!

—John Denver

Prologue

Nineteen seventy-four was a bad time to go crazy. The talk in our townhouse complex in Virginia Beach was of the Stockholm Syndrome, the Hearst kidnapping, Watergate, and what the government had done to Martha Mitchell. "I had Viet Cong hold guns to my head, but I never proposed," spat one Navy man whenever talk turned to the young women in the Stockholm bank robbery who married their captors.

The story I stuck on was Patty's. That spring the famous photo of Patty Hearst appeared. Citizen Tania's image was everywhere, her fine soft face turned tough. The beret; her warrior stance; the way she held the butt of the carbine against her pelvis—everything about her thrilled me. I studied the photos of Patty and Tania like reverse before and after pictures from a Mary Kay makeover. Was there any princess left in Tania's eyes? I secretly hoped she hadn't been brainwashed and that the kidnapping had been a fortunate excuse to abandon her rich-girl life. I imagined Tania as Annie Oakley, the only other woman I'd seen pictured with a gun. In my eight-year-old mind, Patty was a female Robin Hood. She'd left her palace and come over to our side. Folks laughed when Patty's father was forced to spend his riches to feed the hungry in California and then whined he'd go broke in the process.

"Don't you believe everything you hear, Gingie," my father said as we watched the evening news. He put his big freckled arm around my neck and whispered in my ear, "That man can afford to buy the world a Coke."

My mother, on the other hand, identified with the loud-mouthed Martha Mitchell, the attorney general's wife, who seemed to have walked straight out of a gin-soaked Tennessee Williams play set in the drawing rooms of Watergate era Washington, D.C., Martha, with her blonde bouffant and silk dresses, was the visual opposite of my mother, whose long black hair and black eyes made her look something of a hybrid between Liz Taylor and Cher. When the topic turned to Watergate and the Mitchells, people waved Martha off as "that crazy Southerner." But my loudmouthed mother admired and defended Martha as much as I loved Tania and when it later came out that Martha wasn't hallucinating, that she had truly been drugged in a hotel room by the FBI, my mother felt vindicated right along with her. "I'm with you, Martha baby!" my mother exclaimed. "We know the truth, don't we? We'll show 'em." She'd lift her dewy glass of Gallo white and salute the television. "Amen, amen," she murmured and ticked her fingernails against her wineglass.

I wanted to be Citizen Tania; my mother wanted to be

Martha Mitchell. It wouldn't be long before we both got our wish.

*   *   *

One year after Patty Hearst robbed Hibernia National Bank, my mother lost her mind and kidnapped [kidnapped] my sister and me to our family cottage in Kechotan, Virginia.

Her reason was simple. My mother believed she had been inducted into a secret army. My mother, my baby sister, Emma, and I were foot soldiers entrusted with setting up a field hospital.

We lived in that cottage for over three years.

2000

*L*et me start with some history. Mother had just turned thirty-two when the first signs of schizophrenia sprouted in her brain. In terms of the disease, which usually strikes people in their late teens and early twenties, she was a late bloomer. In 1974 my mother had her first psychotic break—I was eight, my sister one, and my father thirty-six. Over five years with active psychosis would pass before she was seen by a psychiatrist early in 1981, hospitalized for four weeks, diagnosed, medicated, and sent home. But by then, her disease had progressed to a stage of severity that would limit effective treatment. Ultimately, this resulted in her permanent institutionalization.

"How could this happen?" This is the refrain I have heard from friends and head-shaking shrinks over the years.

"In an educated, middle-class family?"

"With children at stake?"

"Why didn't anybody *do* anything?"

"How is this possible?"

I was just busy trying to get through those years—these were questions I had never had time to ask. For many years I certainly had no answer other than a blank shrug.

In my 33rd year, I began asking my parents and sister and friends about the years my family was held hostage by my mother's delusions. Now when someone says, "Why couldn't somebody help you?" I can say in reply:

"Here's how. Sit back. Listen. It could happen to you."

1974

The spring before my mother's first psychotic episode we lived in a town house in a complex of town houses and apartments in Virginia Beach. My father worked in a bank in Portsmouth, Virginia; my mother was stay-at-home wife and mom. My sister was one year old and in a half-body cast to correct her displaced hips, a congenital defect. One day I came home from third grade to find my mother in the den, bent over the sofa, frantically changing my sister's diaper through the large square cut in the gray eggy-smelling crotch of the cast. Mother had her red, polka-dot scarf knotted in her hair and was dressed in a wool dress I'd never seen before. It had blue stripes and little brass buttons embossed with anchors. Her white nylon gloves, reserved for church or weddings, were laid out beside her purse on the foyer table.

"There's a treasure hunt," she told me. "We need to go." I

wondered if this was like the scavenger hunts I'd gone on at birthday parties.

"What do we have to get?"

"It's a different kind of treasure hunt. We need to follow the color red. It will lead us there." She put on her lipstick in the hall mirror by holding the golden tube against her bottom lip and turning her head from side to side. She grimaced to wipe a red smear from her teeth.

"Where?" I demanded. "To the party?"

My mother paused and looked confused. She set her hand on her purse and looked as if she might cry. My sister burbled from the floor. Mother suddenly twisted her head and shoulders straight—she had a lovely erect carriage, like Patricia Neal. "To the most magnificent place," she said mysteriously, and her black eyes darkened. A line of electric thrill ran up my legs and back. Mother hauled my sister up and tried to arrange her yellow ruffled skirt to cover the cast. I grabbed my mother's purse and gloves from the foyer, and we were off.

In the car we followed the color red. Until I started looking, I'd never noticed before how many things were red. Stop signs, other cars, billboards, fire hydrants. We drove and drove until we were in the neighboring city of Chesapeake. We drove until my excitement faded. My sister drained her bottle of formula, and she began to drool and chewed idly on the bottle's brown nipple. My mother's scarf slipped from her head.

"When are we going to get there?"

"I don't know," she snapped.

"I want to go home. This is stupid." We were far down a

long, newly paved road. Just then I saw a sign. WELCOME TO CHESAPEAKE POINTE. Red balloons were tethered to a red-lettered sign. "This is it!" I screamed. My mother paused at the white split-rail fence and squinted at the sign.

"It may be," she conceded. We drove in.

Chesapeake Pointe was a community of fancy town homes built on man-made hills. There were no real hills in Virginia Beach and I imagined that this place was built on a hill of bottles and cans, like Mount Trashmore, the local go-cart track. When we pulled into the parking lot, we were greeted by two sales reps, a tiny blonde woman with blood-red nails and lips to match, and a man whose distinguishing feature was his missing arm. Vietnam, I guessed. They filled my mother's hands with flyers and floor plans and then ushered us inside the town homes.

The rooms echoed; the ceilings soared. The furniture, walls, and floors were white and shimmery. I hoisted my sister on my hip, or rather, against my hip—her cast held her legs apart in a rigid upside-down U and her feet were held apart by a spreader bar—and we found the kids' room.

All the furniture was pressed against the walls and the Sahara white carpet invited you to fall to the floor and crawl across it, which is exactly what Enona and I did. I had stopped looking for red when I discovered an enormous plastic treasure chest, filled with plastic toys in plastic wrappers and a roll of jewel-colored lollipops sealed in cellophane that endlessly unfurled. While the grown-ups were in the hallway I stuffed my pockets. My mother walked in the room and shot me a look. I stuck a lollipop in my mouth. Red, of course.

"We need to go now," she said.

"We just got here!" I whined. Then, low, "Did you find the treasure?"

She looked embarrassed or mad, or both. The man beside her kept talking. Her foot began to rock. She was wearing the most marvelous shoes—blue suede clogs with a three-inch cork wedge. They looked like little boats that could be docked in a marina. "Where do you currently reside? Will you be relocating to Chesapeake soon?" The sales rep fixed his one hand to my mother's shoulder and she was bending her knees and twisting her body in order to disengage him. I hoisted my sister off the floor and my mother bent down and seized my hand and literally pulled me out of the house. The sales rep followed us to the car and continued his pitch. She didn't say anything and refused to look at him.

She opened the door and he blocked her by leaning into the door frame with his one arm. "Look here, lady, don't waste my time. I'm here for people who are interested in buying. You got me, lady? I'm no tour guide." Then he looked at me in disgust—a look that would become increasingly familiar in the years to come. At that time I was thinking that look meant he was going to take back the lollipops, but he merely sneered as we got in the car and drove down the long hill and out the gates of Chesapeake Pointe.

Rush hour traffic had set in, and the roadways were otherworldly. A rippled haze of exhaust made the pavement float and buckle, and the taillights of the chain of cars flashed and jerked like a slow-moving Chinese dragon. My mother's face crumpled on itself and her hands trembled.

My sister, who was normally placid, began to cry. I un-

wrapped a yellow lollipop for her and she sucked on it between sobs until she fell asleep, her sticky hand jammed in
her mouth, the lollipop tangled in her hair.

We turned onto a four-lane byway and the car in front of
us stopped without warning. My mother slammed on the
brakes and she began crying in earnest and so hard that she
turned off at the next exit and pulled over to the side of the
road. She didn't speak. I handed Mom a green lollipop. "I
know the way," I lied. "Let me tell you." I was tired and scared
and I wanted to go home and yet I was sure I could find our
way back. Mom stared out the window, and I could tell she
wasn't really looking at anything. Then I saw that she was
looking at the empty reflection of herself in the glass. I took
the lollipop back from my mother, unwrapped it, and handed
it back to her.

"We go down this road on field trips. I'll tell you how to
get there." She blankly turned the key and started driving. I
began looking for signposts of my own. The pink dairy building—turn here, I said. Then the Esso billboard—soon things
really did begin to look familiar. There was the Be-Lo, the
road my dentist's office was on, there was our town home
complex, there was our town house. My mother pulled into
our parking space and slumped at the wheel, pale. I was full
of myself, so pleased I had found our way home.

My father was waiting on the stoop, one hand jammed in
the front pocket of his Levi's, the other fishing dead bugs out
of the front porch light. I leapt out of the car. "We were lost
on our treasure hunt, but I found our way home! All by myself!" He looked at me, puzzled, and walked over to where

my mother now stood, tears streaming down her face. My father unstrapped my sleeping sweaty sister and handed her to me.

"What's wrong? What's happened?" he asked my mother. They leaned their heads together and he cupped the back of her head with his hand. "Oh, Nathan," I heard her wail. And she began to sob and sob.

Later, I remember her being in bed and my father telling me that she was sick. I said she was sad and confused and Dad said those things could sometimes make a person sick. My eight-year-old mind reasoned she was sad because the adventure had turned out so badly; because there had been no magnificent place or reward for following the color red.

Now I know she was sad and scared for a different reason—she was having a delusion, and she knew she was having a delusion. She was disintegrating into madness, but she wasn't so far gone, yet, that she wasn't fighting it. Her tears were proof of that.

2000

*D*o you remember the first time you heard the voices?" I ask my mother. We're sitting beside a small fishpond in the Catholic nursing home where she now lives. I've just now started asking questions of my parents. For many years my mother has been too fragile and my father has flatly refused to discuss the past, but things have changed. My mother is relatively stable and my father has agreed to try to answer my questions.

My mother's gaze is fixed on the orange flashes of the Japanese carp in the water. I've come to this visit just so I can ask this one question and the mere thought of asking it provokes a fear that raises the hair on my arms.

"The very first time you heard the voices, do you remember when it was?" I blurt it out, unable to bear the weight inside me any longer.

She turns her face to me and smiles, exposing the wide lazy gap between her front teeth. "Oh yes." I feel my breath halt.

Mother rests her hand on my arm. Her fingers look just like mine, small, but not shapely. The backs of her hands are dry and wrinkled; her palms a tight pink that looks almost polished. "It was the most glorious day. We were living in Virginia Beach. I went to the cleaners to drop off your father's shirts."

"What did the voices say? Were they scary voices?"

"No. The voices told me to drop off your father's shirts at the cleaners. They said, 'You've got a good-looking husband. Take his shirts to the cleaners.'" I laugh; I can't help it. I've been terrified of asking this question, thinking it might trigger something horrible in my mother or me and I expected the voices to say horrible things, unnerving things. Something as strangely ordinary as "Take his shirts to the cleaners" never crossed my mind. Then she holds out her hand in front of her as a shield. "But the colors. Oh, Gawd!"

Schizophrenics often see auras around colors and objects. For my mother it was red. For Van Gogh it was the stars in the night sky.

"So the voices didn't bother you? They didn't scare you."

"Not until later," she says and pulls her long graying hair off her neck. "It's too hot out here. I need to go back to my room." Visit over. Class dismissed.

1975

*T*o our friends and neighbors in Virginia Beach our disappearance must have appeared to be the typical domestic variety—a now you see them, now you don't sort of affair. What must they have wondered? Was Mother's leaving some flash of whimsy? A longing for liberation? After all, it was the age of Betty Friedan angst and women on TV and in magazines were breaking the yoke of twentieth-century wifedom, getting divorces and jobs.

Our abduction, however, was wholly unlike Patty Hearst's clear-cut and dramatic departure from domestic life. In Patty's world there were good guys and bad guys, but then the bad guys turned out to be kind of cool. "Urban guerrillas." It was like the stories of people kidnapped by Indians who decided to stay and become part of the tribe. Anyway, until my mother told us, my sister and I hadn't a clue we were being kidnapped. I simply came home from school one afternoon and my mother told me we were going to our cottage in Kechotan for a couple of days. She said my father would join us there.

I recall asking only one question: "You sure you know how to get there?" I asked not only because of Mother's recent tendency to forget where she was, but because she had driven to the cottage by herself just once before, the previous winter, to put camellias on her mother's grave. Though it was only an hour and a half's drive to Kechotan, it was a much longer trip than my mother was used to taking. She had learned to drive only four years before.

"Would you get in the car, Miss Smart Aleck!" She swatted at me with her straw hat. I dropped my book bag inside the front door and did as she said. There was nothing in her manner that made me uneasy. I do recall that she seemed especially happy. I suppose because she suddenly had a purpose, a job, a mission. Though I didn't realize it at the time, the voices that had at first told her to drop my father's shirts off at the cleaners were now telling her that she had been chosen to help serve her country in a secret war. Her mission was to set up a field hospital at the cottage. Hundreds of orphaned children would travel to our cottage at night. We were to treat their injuries and evacuate them to safety.

But right then, getting into the car, I knew none of that. I just sang along with the songs on the radio as we drove out of Virginia Beach. Our dog Ralph hung his huge gray head out of the passenger's side window, his drool streaking across the back window of the Beetle. His tail thumped up and down and Emma tried to grab it in her little hands. Our cat, Oliver, dug in under my mother's seat and yowled.

"Good-bye, Oyster Pointe Village," my mother called as we

left our townhouse court. "Good-bye, pool. Good-bye, Be-Lo. Good-bye, Tammie Sugarman's house." Good-bye, good-bye. She was ecstatic. I became caught up in my mother's farewell litany and shouted out good-bye to every billboard and hitchhiker and seagull until I was giddy beyond calling.

When we hit the Hampton Roads Tunnel, John Denver was singing "Thank God I'm a Country Boy" and my mother sang louder and harder than I had ever seen, waving her head in the wind, laughing so hard tears squeezed out of the corners of her eyes. Emma was in the backseat, clapping her hands and growling, her latest trick. She sounded like a puppy.

"Here we go, Gingie," my mother announced as we descended into the mouth of the tunnel. I held my breath and began to count to see how long I could last. The car went dark, the radio signal disappeared and we went under.

Part One

Kechotan, Virginia

1975

We are inside the tunnel. It's a filthy place, like a big yellow-tiled bathroom with soot on the walls and bad lighting. I wonder if the tunnel ever leaks and how I will get out if it begins to flood. I imagine crabs burrowing between the bricks of the tunnel and speedboats zooming over top of us. I imagine that the tunnel has detached from the bridges and we are really floating underwater like the lost island of Atlantis.

I never make it past 68 because my chest burns and aches. I gasp in a scorching mouthful of air. My cousin Darby can hold her breath to 102 and I am determined to beat her or pass out trying.

It isn't until we are almost out of the tunnel that we see light and the exit up onto the other side of the bridge. The radio magically pops back on, and I turn around. I am amazed to look back over the wide green bay. We were just deep under all that water, able to breathe. My sister is asleep.

"Emma's asleep," I tell my mother.

"She must've thought it was night inside the tunnel."

On the other side of the tunnel the mood in the car changes. Mother clicks the radio off. We are silent as we drive into Kechotan, the town where my grandmother grew up, and onto the land where my grandfather had built her this cottage out of shipyard scraps.

Like many Southern families, decades of relative poverty have only served to increase the family pride. King Charles I of England granted the land on which the cottage is built —my mother's ancestors were landed gentry. My mother's family can—and unfortunately often dose—trace themselves back to Kechotan to pre-Revolutionary War times.

Every trip to Kechotan my mother tells me, "You were born of pioneers and pirates." As a child I imagined the pioneers in tricornered hats. I thought the pirates were the doubloon and parrot-shouldered variety. Later I'd understand the pioneers were cattle farmers who drove their herd across the marsh at low tide to eat and mate and the pirates were common thieves, their booty nothing more exotic than salt pork.

Soon we pull up the long driveway and get out of the car. Ralph bounds away after some quail in the brush. Here there is no sound of another car or other people. The air smells scrubbed and clean when wind blows through the bank of bayberry trees near the marsh. Cicadas hiss from the pines.

Mother opens the combination lock that secures the house —twenty-four-thirty-six-twenty-six. The smell that pours from the cottage is cool and dank, like the smooth underside of a garden rock.

I set my sister on her blanket under a pine tree with a box

of graham crackers and her favorite toy, an avocado-green plastic flour scoop. Though she was out of her cast, she wasn't walking or crawling much and could be trusted not to go far.

The cottage is a tiny place—a seven-hundred-square-foot cabin constructed by my grandfather for short-term summer inhabitancy. Its foundation is two inches of poured cement that also serves as the floor. The metal shower stall was purchased at a battleship auction. The front door handle is an elbowed pine branch. A curious fact: The house has no ceilings. The tops of the walls end where regular walls stop, but above them is two to three feet of space and unpainted rafters. The previous summer I had discovered how to hitch my foot on the door handle of my room, pull myself to the tops of the wooden walls and balance myself astride the walls in the house—one leg in my parents' bedroom, the other in the living room. The perfect perch to spy.

"First," my mother declares, "we have been ordered to sanitize the premises." She opens the hood of the Volkswagen and pulls out buckets and bottles of ammonia.

My mother shakes out several bandannas from her bag and ties one kerchief-style on my head. Then she does the same for Emma. "There." She says it with relief and satisfaction, as if she's just put the finishing touch on the *Mona Lisa*.

"What do you mean 'we've been ordered'? Who ordered us?"

"That's for me to know, missy. You just do as you're told. You take orders or they'll court-martial you and put you in jail. And I am your superior."

My mother has never spoken quite this way before and it jars me. I suddenly feel trapped between thick walls of glass.

Her words are as strong to me as a blow to my face, but they also have an unexpected narcotic quality that temporarily eliminates the heat in my body and evaporates my soul. On any other day I wouldn't hesitate to fight her, but today, I do as I am told.

I say to myself: She is your mother. You will do as you are told.

Inside the cottage cobwebs thick and ropy with dust hang under tabletops and shelves; birds nest in the rafters. There are old crab shells and minnow husks in the corners, from last fall's floods. Mother and I throw sitting covers over the sofa and chairs and set Emma down with a few toys.

We haul the mattresses from the bunk beds into the sun to bleach out the mildew. Then Mother cuts up all of her underpants and we scrub the floors down with ammonia and clean the windows with vinegar and newspaper until they sparkle. Mom unpacks two small cans of paint and two new brushes and we carefully paint the glass of each window in the cottage solid black. "Now," Mom says, "it's like our very own secret hideout. When we're here at night, we can have the lights on and no one will know."

I wonder how much turpentine it is going to take to clean the windows again.

My cousin Darby runs down from her house two acres over. My mother's brother, Chuck, built his house on his share of the family property just to the north of us. To our south is the home of my dead grandmother's sister, Pearline. She keeps to herself, like all the old-timers in Kechotan. She almost never talks to us, but she brings over things from her garden. I hardly know a soul in town who isn't kin.

"Are you down for the weekend?" Darby asks me. Mom is in the bathroom, arranging the shelves. "Can you play?" Darby is eleven, just two years older than me, but she looks even older. She's thick-legged and freckled, and with her short shorts and bandanna halter top, she could easily pass for fourteen. I toss my broom and dustpan in the corner and head out the door the way I always do when we're down at the cottage for a weekend, but Mom comes after us.

"Darby, we've important work to do today and Gingie must stay here to care for young Emma. I'm so sorry." My mother is speaking with a British accent all of a sudden. We think she's making a joke and so Darby and I crack up and keep going. Mother grabs my arm and begins walking me back to the house. I must be putting up a good fight, because she's got me underneath my arms and is pulling me backward through the pine needles. I can see the path of my drug feet and I can tell I'm kicking: there's wormy black earth turned up from where my heels strike. Darby starts crying and yells at my mother and then flees for her house. Once we're inside the cottage, Mom bolts the door.

"Can't you see what we have to do? Other people will not understand. You cannot talk about the secret war. We are on a mission. You have been called to help. This is very important. Your government has asked you to help. You will do what I say."

There are tears and fighting and I vow to myself I will try to get out of the cottage by pretending I'm asleep and then sneaking out.

Caught, I feel Mother wrap her arms around me and even though I struggle to get free I can't.

"I love you, you know that, I would never do this if I didn't love you. You must help. This is important. You will understand."

* * *

I must have cried myself to sleep in her arms because this is where I wake an hour later. Mom is asleep too. Her arms still circle me, her chest half on top of me, and I push her off. She rolls to the other side of the bed. I am exhausted, but no longer scared. Washed out is how I feel.

Mother's room is filthy from the winter dampness; mildew climbs the walls in pink-and-black-speckled streaks, like it's made of flesh. The floors are damp and slick with condensation. It's going to take more than ammonia to sanitize this place.

I find Emma playing in the other bedroom. She's scattered and crushed her graham crackers across the floor and I take her into the bathroom to wash the crust of crumbs off her face. (I pick her up.) Her Pampers slide from her legs and hit the floor with a wet slap—they're as full as a milk carton.

2000

Should I recall this time as horrifying? I don't. At the time my mother's actions and behavior were incomprehensible; there was no context in which I could place the bizarre events that were occurring. Those moments became suspended in my mind in the amber of the present tense—so that's how I will tell it here. For years, whenever I would try to recall an event from the years at the cottage that moment would consume me, flood me, almost as if I were there again. There's another thing: There was never a clear delineation between my mother sane and my mother mad—a place where I could say this was my mother before, this is my mother after. Unlike the conversion of Patty into Tania, there were no pictures to study. There was no reason why. There was no one to blame.

If there was ever a moment when "things changed," the move to Kechotan was it. At the time, I honestly believed that I could run away if I wanted, like the war children my mother expected. I could be an orphan. Of course, I didn't run away, I stayed. And because I stayed I thought it meant I wanted to stay. Even at the age of nine, staying with my mother felt like a choice. Once I had made that choice, I was with my mother in her mission to set up the hospital. I decided that I would believe in the secret war. My mother's delusion became my delusion; not so much a choice as a simple fact. It was a way not to lose her, yes, but I guess it was also more fun for an nine-year-old tomboy to believe she was chosen to aid in a secret war than to believe she was being held hostage by her mother.

I had my own desires, but I purposefully kept them small. That first night at the cottage, I scratched through the paint on one of my windowpanes so I could check outside whenever I liked to see when it was day or night. No light was to escape from the cottage at night—Mom said it could give away our coordinates to the enemy—so during the day, I kept the shade down so she wouldn't see what I'd done. The second day I made the stars. With a small nail, I copied the Pleiades just as they appeared in my mythology book. Sometimes at night, bright moonlight would filter through and there the sisters would be, glowing on the cement floor. Some nights, just before I fell asleep, I'd wonder what happened to the seventh sister and where she hid.

1975

*O*ur third day at the cottage we walk to my Aunt Lisa's house to use the phone. Mom calls and informs my father that she has every intention of spending the summer in Kechotan and that he can join us if he wishes. Then she's quiet. I assume that Dad is talking on the other end. But all I hear is her breathing and what she doesn't say. She doesn't tell him about the secret mission she's on. She doesn't tell him that she has no intention of ever moving back to Virginia Beach. Mom hangs up the phone and sets fifty cents on the counter for my aunt.

"It's fine, Molly," Aunt Lisa says and scoots the quarters back to her with her long bony fingers. "You're family." She smiles at me. I like Lisa; she is kind, though reserved, and her house is always clean and good-smelling. Everything my cousins wear she sews by hand. She even makes her own candles.

"You're not my family. You're just my brother's wife."

Mom laughs a big **HA.** "What a load of crap." If I close my eyes and pretend I'm watching television, I'd swear it was Martha Mitchell. But it's my mother doing her best imitation.

Aunt Lisa slowly steps back from the counter as if she thinks my mother can walk through it. Darby and her big sister, sheila, appear in the doorway. The heavy glass wall falls between me and the world.

"Molly," my aunt ventures, "I don't know what's going on here, but I consider you family. I love you."

"You can go to hell," my mother says. "I don't love you." Aunt Lisa's face reddens and her eyes go all watery. Darby and her sister run to their mother and begin to cry. "I see no point in lying to each other."

"What's the matter, Mom?" they cry. "What's happening?"

Mother shoves the fifty cents in her pocket and makes sure to slam the door behind her. I wonder if my cousins will ever speak to me again and who I will play with. "Now we can work in peace," Mother says as we walk back to the cottage. "They won't be bothering us."

2000

Mother and Father had always had a tempestuous relationship and she was prone to fits of rage followed by wailing apology. She was used to getting what she wanted when she wanted it. My grandmother Virginia had seen to that.

According to my father, my grandmother was of that breed of Southerner who though poor and working class put on airs of lost aristocracy. My aristocratic grandmother had been, in real life, a beautician who married a South Carolina merchant marine when she was in her early thirties. Hardly a wedding of note.

My grandmother's pall of lost fortune and class stayed with her and she determined that her daughter would have the fine life that she didn't get. There were ballet lessons, fine clothes and jewelry, charm school and cotillion, all of which took their toll on the family finances and required sacrifices of everyone else.

My father describes my mother's house as a tiny two-bedroom home with worn furniture and a sad feel, except for my mother's bedroom, which was decorated with a new mahogany canopy bed and fine lace curtains. Her dresser was topped with Chanel perfumes and filigreed silver boxes and she had a closet full of new perfectly tailored clothes each season.

It was surreal, as if my mother lived in a different house from the rest of her family. And what my grandmother had haplessly hoped for, that my mother would marry well and restore her family's social standing, cultivated little more than a sense of selfish entitlement that stayed with my mother permanently. If my mother had decided to relocate from Virginia Beach to the moon without a moment's notice to anyone, including her children, it wouldn't have been out of character.

It was in this way my mother's early delusions went unnoticed and then ignored those first few months at the cottage. After all, she had never been a woman you could reason with.

2000

*M*y mother's delusions were big. Little delusions and small insanities are unfortunate, yet common things. The persistent thought that your coworkers are talking about you behind your back; the compulsion that bids you to touch the doorknob twelve times before leaving your house; the unrelenting desire to slice your own flesh—these conditions, troubling as they might be, won't get you a seat in the waiting room with someone like my mother.

Schizophrenics hear voices. Now understand that unlike the voice you hear in your head telling you to remember to take your child to soccer practice at five o'clock, these voices, though they come from the brain, sound as if they come from outside. These voices are as loud and unpredictable as someone else's stereo. It's not like being possessed; it's like being assaulted and enslaved.

Imagine, like my mother, that these voices start telling you there's a war, and that you have been chosen to set up a field hospital. Perhaps you believe what the voices tell you. Or maybe you do what they say because sometimes when you do—the voices stop and you get your head back.

Setting up a field hospital is a massive task when you have a troop of soldiers trained and equipped. My mother planned to do it with me and my baby sister as helpers. The task is alarming in its scope—and quite impressive.

When she wasn't delusional my mother was too distracted to have so much as mercurochrome and Band-Aids in the house at the same time. But one of the remarkable thing about delusions is how they make you focus and how they drive you.

Of course, I didn't understand any of this at the time, nor did my mother, so we took the first step toward setting up the field hospital: We drove into town and went shopping.

1975

I thought we were going to Newport News," I say when Mom pulls into the parking lot of Gaffney's. "You said we were going to Penney's." Gaffney's is the only place in Kechotan like a department store. A cheap department store. GET IT AT GAFFNEY'S, the sign reads, FOR LESS.

"This is fine," Mom says, and checks her lipstick in the rearview. She looks back at Emma, playing with her chiming apple toy on the backseat floor. "Stay here, Emma Byrd. Don't talk to anyone." My sister keeps rocking the apple toy in response. Mom cracks the back windows and locks her in the car.

I've got one last chance before she goes in the store. "Mom, people know us here. Do you want them to find out? Let's go to Newport News." My throat feels suddenly sore.

"This is fine. You don't need to worry," she says. "I know what I'm doing." She straightens her shoulders and raises her chin, then swings open the door. I follow.

I walk past Mrs. Moody at the register and say hi. She nods. Mom is looking through the winter jackets that are lined up against one wall.

"Those're on sale," Mrs. Moody calls out. "Fifteen dollars each. Leftovers from last year."

"That's too good a price," Mom whispers to me. "And we need coats for the children."

"Edith, ring out thirty-five coats for me."

Mrs. Moody snorts a little laugh and waves her hand. Mom sticks out her chin and marches over to the checkout counter. "I said I'd like thirty-five of the children's coats and I'd like thirty-five of the children's shoes."

Cap'n Liss and his wife are now behind Mom in line. Cap'n Liss is ninety-two and he still drives, though he goes so slow folks drive around him. He turns his head to look at Mom and then he, Mrs. Liss, and Mrs. Moody all look over at me. I feel hot and look at my shoes.

"What're you going to do with thirty-five jackets, Molly Roberts?"

Mom smiles. She's been expecting this question. "Why they're for charity, Edith." Mom draws out Dad's BankAmericard from her wallet and lays it on the countertop. She knows how to get what she wants.

Mrs. Moody looks down at the BankAmericard for a long time. Then she snaps it up to her cash register. "Well, you got to pick out the ones you want. I've got to mash in the stock numbers."

"Pick out the shoes, Gingie," Mom says. She walks over to the rack of coats and begins ripping off tags. I can't move. No one in the store is moving except my mother. I think about my room in Virginia Beach with its ceiling and a door that locks the quiet in. I think about starting school in Virginia Beach in brand-new clothes. I think about telling Dad.

Mrs. Moody sets down a cardboard box for the shoes and touches my hair. "It's O.K., sweet," she whispers.

I snap my head away from her and grab the box. "I've already got a mother," I tell her and walk over to the shoes. I don't even bother to count; I just fill up the box till it's full. Then I drag it across the floor to her checkout lane. Mrs. Moody rings us out. She looks at the total and sucks her breath in through her teeth, then she sets the reciept in front of mem like a dare.

Mom signs the receipt in one casual stroke.

"You don't forget those jackets, Molly."

Mom walks out the door with an enormous pile of coats sliding in her arms to put in the back of the Volkswagen.

"Aren't you going to count the shoes?" I ask Mrs. Moody. "Don't you want the stock numbers?"

"I trust you, Gingie," she says, and crinkles her eyes at me. The heat in my head fills my chest and legs. I feel light and thick at the same time.

I reach down on the candy rack and dump an entire shelf box of Zotz lemon candy on top of the shoes. My ears are dull with my pulse. I look back up at Mrs. Moody and then pour in the grape Zotz as well. Now I'm shaking.

"You paying for those?"

I take the edge of the box of shoes and drag it out the door. Mom puts it in the car. She doesn't even notice the candy.

I know I'm in for it. Once when I was with Dad I saw Mrs. Moody grab one of the kids from Messick, the poor side of

Kechotan, by his ear until he turned over a Sugar Daddy he'd swiped. "Good for you," Dad'd told her. But now she doesn't move.

"Go get the last bunch of coats," Mom tells me and starts the car. I push the door open and gather the last six jackets in my arms. Cap'n Liss is talking in his high quavery voice. "That Molly never has lived up to her family's name."

Mrs. Moody looks right in my eyes as I back out the door.

"Mmm-hmmm," she says. "Her girl's gonna be just like her."

1992

*M*y husband, Curry, and I have been married a year and a half. We live in a huge rented farmhouse, complete with a green-painted tin roof, bead board walls, and an old fouled well. We find this place wildly romantic. We are twenty-four years old.

When we wake in the mornings, we dress in front of the space heater and then head to the kitchen. Our Siberian husky whines over her bowl, and with a metal spoon we smash the thin layer of ice that glazes her water dish so that she can drink. After sharing a shower (a daily necessity because the hot water heater takes two hours between uses to fully warm), my husband drives to Duke University where he is pursuing his Ph.D. in computer science and I climb the stairs to the attic rooms to write. I've recently quit my first job and have no prospects for another.

In the attic, I can barely work. I write a bit, listen to classical music on the radio, look out of the window at the scummy pond across the way. I read what I have written and then lie on the floor, hoping to fall asleep. I go downstairs and turn on the TV and watch a game show. I am appalled that I know the lyrics to the Huggies' Pull-Up jingle. I go back upstairs determined to try to write again. A small space opens in the bad space and I work for almost an hour without distraction. What pulls me out of my writing are voices. I hear people laughing. Not loudly, but heartily, and at a great distance. I've always known it would happen and I have always been terrified it would happen: my mother's voices blossoming in my head. My mother's illness becoming my illness.

I move around the room, trying to find where the tiny voices reside. I listen in the corners, press my ears against the walls, look outside to make sure it is not music from a car. I cover my face, sit on the floor, and breathe. I press my fists against my eyes until dizzy spirals of light appear.

"I amnotcrazyIamnotcrazyIamnotcrazy," I insist. "IamnotcrazyIamnotcrazy." Thinking will make a thing so, I hope, but when I stop chanting and uncover my eyes, the voices are still there. Dread pours through me, I feel queasy. Of course it's happening. Schizophrenia is bred in the bone. It's my turn is all.

I start crying. I pull my hair until my scalp burns. Then, in an idiot's attempt to block out the voices, I cover my ears. Once my sobs subside, I realize the voices are gone. I uncover my ears: the voices return. I cover my ears again: nothing! I uncover them: a new sound, like rustling paper. Another sound, a sudden static pop. My radio light is on and the tuning dial is half a measure off to some ghostly version of my favorite classical station. It's the radio. I start laughing and crying, turning up the dial until it resists. Leonard Bernstein has just been introduced, the applause fades back, there's a faint knocking in the background, and Beethoven's Ninth Symphony begins.

1975

At the cottage Mother and I pack the coats into green plastic garbage bags and set them beside the provisions. She lines the shoes on the long shelves above the stove and sink, and when they fill, on top of the refrigerator.

"These're really cute, and they're size fives," Mom says, and dangles a pair of maroon lace-ups that don't fit in her lineup.

"I don't want them."

"What's the matter with these? They're adorable."

"No way."

"Put them in your closet. Those are your new shoes and you'll wear them when I say so."

"I'll put them in my closet but I will not wear them."

"You'll wear them now if I tell you to wear them now, missy."

She's mad at me for nothing. Mad because she got all nervous at Gaffney's. She used to get mad at Dad but now I'm it all the time.

"I'm not putting those shoes in my closet, because I'm not ever going to wear them."

"You'll—"

"No, I will not," I yell, and walk out of the cottage.

Mother catches the screen door before it can slam. "Where are you going?"

I keep walking toward Chuck and Lisa's and don't turn around.

"You know the rules," she calls after me. I wave her off.

I'm allowed to pretty much do as I please most afternoons as long as I follow the rules, which isn't hard, because there are only two. Rule number one is don't tell anyone about the secret war. Rule number two is in the cottage before dark.

There are no kids here to play with except my cousins and most evenings and weekends Uncle Chuck has them working. He wanted boys, he always says that, but Darby and Sheila work harder than any boys I know. They lift boulders and push wheelbarrows full of wet concrete for Uncle Chuck's seawall. They clean fish and pick crabs on the pier. Sometimes Sheila cries, but not Darby. Sheila wants long fingernails and nail polish. But she's not allowed for three more years when she's fifteen. Still, she collects the stuff. She even has a little mirrored tray in her bedroom arranged with twenty little tester lipsticks that the Avon lady has given to her. They look like an army of cigarette butts. Sometimes when I'm up there she'll open up the tops and we'll stare at all the shimmery pink, red, and brown triangles. Then she'll close them all up. She's not allowed to wear lipstick either.

Chuck and Lisa's house is on higher land than our cottage and it overlooks the cove. I can usually tell if somebody is home because the living room and the dining room behind it both have large glass windows, so you can see through the entire house out to the water. Their shiny black wood door is always locked and I have to ring the bell to get in. Most afternoons Sheila and Aunt Lisa lie on the polished wood floor and play hearts, while Darby watches television. But today is different. Uncle Chuck is home, and a man he works with is in the hospital.

"I heard them say his bones were all broken and sticking out of his skin. He hit the bottom so hard his eyes shot out of his head and his feet were smoking."

"That's a lie! A gross, gross lie. How can you say such things, Darby Phillips? Don't you believe her, Gingie. She's just a big, fat liar."

"It's the truth. Mom and Dad don't tell Sheila anything because she's so sen-si-tive."

"It's just machines keeping him alive until Charlene gets there. She was in West Point at her mother's when it happened."

"Mom told me Jimmy slipped. Now his neck is broken." Sheila strokes her throat. "I'll bet he has to be in a wheelchair the rest of his life. But maybe he can learn to draw those pictures for cards with his teeth."

"You are so stupid!" Darby screams.

Sheila just stares at the water and runs her fingernail along the side of her neck.

"You wanna know who's right? C'mon." Darby motions me into the house. Sheila stays by the seawall.

As we walk to the house Darby tells me what has happened. Jimmy was inspecting an aircraft carrier. The ship was still under construction; there was no power. He had a flashlight with him and there were a few lights the welders had strung up and left burning. Everything was routine. Jimmy had been talking to a friend. Then, silence. His buddy turned around to call for Jimmy, shone his flashlight back to see where Jimmy had gone off to. He pointed the beam straight ahead. When he pointed the light to the floor the beam didn't hit anything but a long black fall. The bottom of that ship was so far down that his light couldn't even reach to where Jimmy had fallen. So far down no one even heard him hit.

We creep inside the house and crouch on the stairs trying to listen to Chuck, but we can't hear anything. Aunt Lisa finds us crouched on the stairs and gives us a wicked look. "You know better than this," she whispers in a sharp voice. "Get out of here. Can't you see, your father . . .?"

I look at Darby, her stare so hard she doesn't even blink.

"Don't make me mad, girls."

"Jimmy's gonna die, idn't he?" Darby says, like it's fact.

Lisa pulls hard on her hair and sighs. Her face twists and she looks like she's about to cry herself. "Sometimes girls, death is a blessing. Jimmy's brain and body are broken beyond fixing or healing. The sooner he dies, the better it will be for everyone."

"You never liked Jimmy," Darby says out of nowhere, her eyes and mouth bunching up. "I'll bet you just can't wait for him to die."

"Darby!" The breath rushes out of Lisa and she chokes and sobs as she tries to inhale. I know this much, if I weren't here, things would be different. Aunt Lisa wouldn't waste her time dabbing at her eyes. With one hand she'd have Darby by the scruff of her neck and Uncle Chuck's belt in the other. At least, that's what I've seen.

"You girls get out," Lisa says, and then turns to the little driftwood mirror in the front hall to fix her face. I stand up but Darby just stares at her mother's reflection. Lisa spins around, grabs Darby's shoulders, and pushes her out the front door. Darby goes right back up to the threshold to glare at Lisa but the black door comes at us fast and hard and Aunt Lisa locks it quick behind us.

"What's the matter with you?" I try to catch Darby as she storms back to the seawall. "Huh?"

"Shut up. Just shut up!"

I sit beside Sheila on the seawall and we don't say anything. Darby has a handful of little oyster shells and she tosses them into the water trying to make them skip. Once she skipped a stone five times, but the water's so choppy, the most she's getting now is three.

"You made that up about falling inside the ship," I say. "-That's Grandpa's story."

"Did not."

"Liar. What happened?"

"I don't know. He could have fallen in the ship."

"I thought he fell from a window," Sheila says.

"How do you fall from a window?"

"Well," Sheila says. "Maybe he tripped and the window was open and he just accidentally fell out."

"Maybe."

"Maybe not," says Darby.

When she was eight she said she wanted to die. The she swallowed a bottle of iodine to prove it.

I think of Art Linkletter's daughter, the one who took a hit of acid and thought she could fly, and so flew right out an open window.

"I wonder what it's like to fly," Sheila says and for a long time none of us say's anything else.

*   *   *

"Sun's setting," Darby says and crawls down to the lowest part of the wall, scaring the fiddler crabs back into their holes.

Sheila and I join her and wait as we watch the sun ease itself into a dark blue cloud right above the water's edge. Then, right before the top of the sun disappears, we scramble the twelve feet up to the top of the wall and watch the sunset again. Once when Chuck and Lisa weren't there, Darby and Sheila made the sun set three times by setting a ladder on the side of the house and climbing on to the roof. I imagine if you keep going up, you'd just keep watching the sun go down, but it would never get dark.

"Got to go," I say as we watch the dark rise up through the water and into the sky.

"It's not dark, dark yet." Sheila says.

"Gets dark sooner in the woods." I start walking back. Darby and Sheila just stay put. I have to be in the cottage before dark; they can't go indoors till Lisa calls them.

Right now, at home in Virginia Beach, I'd be out with a pack of twenty other kids, riding my bike over the grassed-up dirt mounds left by the construction workers. I'd ride barefoot until the streetlights flicked on and the sky turned black and parents sent out their older kids to call us in.

When I'd get home, my parents would be on the patio,

laughing, beers or gin and tonics in their hands, citronella candles filling up with black wet moths. My mother would scold me for being so filthy and my father would carry me up to the tub and wash and crème rinse my hair, always careful to make sure nothing got in my eyes. Men like that don't let go unless they die like Jimmy will. Dad'll be calling us back.

*　　*　　*

In Kechotan there are no streetlights. When the sun goes down the spiders come out and spin their sticky nets between the pines. Nothing poisonous, just fat garden spiders that can crawl into your clothes if you tear across one of their webs. Most nights I wave a stick in front of me, so I don't get tangled; but some nights, like tonight, I'll just hold my hands by my side and run face first into the woods, just to see if I'll get caught.

I stop short of our stoop and back up. If you stare at the cottage long enough, you can see little twinkles at the edges of the windowpanes, like tiny Christmas lights. And around the front door and where the roof starts long seams of light escape. We're not exactly invisible.

"Bolt the door," Mom calls from the sofa.

"Mom, do you know that when we have the lights on you can tell there's a house here. Anybody can see it."

"Don't worry. When things start happening we won't have electricity. We'll use oil lanterns and candles. And only when we have to. Did you eat at Lisa's?"

"No."

"They didn't offer you supper?"

"She hadn't fixed it yet."

"Hadn't fixed it? Chuck won't tolerate that."

I take an apple from beside the sink and eat it. Mom has a heap of mending beside her on the sofa. She looks so peaceful, the radio turned low and chiming, her old cookie tin full of needles and old buttons that I stay quiet. Mom dips the needle into an old bar of soap. "Put the seeds in the coffee tin."

I spit the seeds into my palm and blow to dry them off before I drop them in the can. Mom knows what she's doing. Where would you get food when the grocery stores are all blown up and the gardens burned? I never thought the apple I was eating might be the last apple I would ever see. Now I know we can't just toss away whole trees and expect the Richfood will always have what we want. Mom says we will be the ones who know how to provide.

My windbreaker is on Mom's lap and she's sliding the needle quickly through the slippery nylon. "There's nothing wrong with my jacket," I tell her.

"Oh, there's really nothing wrong with most of your clothes. A button here and there. Your posture is another matter."

"What?"

"I'm stitching up your pockets. You're always slumped over like a little old lady. Pockets encourage slouching."

"Do you have to stitch up my coat pockets?" I'm surprised to hear my voice crack. "What if my hands get cold?"

"You have mittens."

"But I usually put them in my pockets. I'll lose them."

"No you won't."

"I will. And then I'll just tear out your stitches!" I yell.

"No," Mom repeats, "you won't."

I snap on the television and whisper, "Yes I will." The set crackles and whines.

"Turn it off," Mom says in a hoarse voice.

"No way." I put my bare feet up on the coffee table and stare at the screen. Mom unplugs the set.

"What are you doing?"

"They've put cameras in there," she whispers. "They're taking pictures."

"There is not a camera in the TV."

"You have no idea." She gets a screwdriver from the kitchen and starts undoing the back of the set. I just stand in the kitchen and watch.

"You're not going to find anything," I call. But already she's pulled off the black plastic shell and is plucking at wires. She reaches in and then hands me a milky glass tube.

"Look at this."

"It's a tube. Dad put it in when the TV broke. All TVs have them."

"But see, it's like a flash cube, all foamy inside. For a special kind of camera."

"Where's the camera?" I ask, trying not to believe her.

"It's in here somewhere. We'll find it. Then we'll have some clues."

Mom has found some other screws inside the TV set to work on. Her whole head is inside the television.

"Sometimes they are very small and disguised." She takes out a wire with a red cap and drops it on the floor.

"Do you think Dad put the camera inside?" I imagine that he's been watching us here the whole time and is waiting for just the right time to take us home.

"No, your father didn't do this."

"He would've seen the camera when he put in the tube."

"Not unless he knew what to look for," Mom says and yanks out three short cords.

"How long till you find the camera?"

"Don't know. Could take a while."

The insides of the set are scattered around her feet.

"How long till you put it back together? I want to watch *The Waltons*."

She's not listening. And I already know the television won't be back together in time for my show.

There's a pot of tomato soup on the stove. "Are you going to eat the rest of this?"

"Go ahead," she says, surveying the parts at her feet.

I turn on the burner and pull the thick skin of the soup to the side of the pot.

"Put on your shoes," Mom calls, and I ignore her. The current isn't grounded and to touch the stove or iron without shoes on sends sharp spangles through your arms and legs. It's not enough to knock you off your feet, like the time I was little and stuck a bobby pin into an outlet, but the current hurts and can take you by surprise.

When I wrap my fingers around the pot handle I feel an electric buzz through my hand and my arm. I can taste a sharp pain in my tongue. "Put on your shoes," Mom says. But I don't move. I'm trying to see how long I can hold on.

1975

*G*et your pack, they're coming." I sit up and Mom is dressed in blue jeans and a dark jacket. Her hair is tucked up under a dark blue bandanna that she has fastened with crisscrossing bobby pins. The clocks read three thirty-three. It's weird to see all the numbers lined up like that, all the same. Maybe I am in a dream, I tell myself, but then the three on the clock flips over to four and I feel my chest and stomach sink together in that tight empty feeling I only have when I'm awake. Mom's wearing new blue tennis shoes that squeak across the cement floor. She opens the refrigerator and puts a Coke in her pack. Television tubes and wires are on the kitchen table.

Something isn't right. The war children aren't coming now, so why is she acting as if they are? But what I say to Mom is, "They're not coming." Flat and plain. I'm learning not to ask questions when I want a clear answer. Every time I ask Mom a question it feels like I fall a little deeper into a hole.

Questions never lead me to answers, only to more questions. And these days the questions that come out of my mouth have too many answers or no real answer at all. I make myself speak carefully, reorder my words, move them around like Scrabble tiles until they come out plain as can be.

"I said they're not coming."

"No," Mom says. "Tonight's a test run. Night maneuvers."

"I don't want to do night maneuvers," I tell her and roll back under covers.

"Oh no you don't. We have to do this tonight. Get your clothes on." Maybe there is something about to happen. Maybe night maneuvers are a good idea. I pull on my brown Toughskins and a green T-shirt. The night air is soft and the half moon lights up the sky.

Mom carries Emma out to the car and lays her in the backseat with her blanket.

"Leave her here, you'll just wake her," I say.

"She'll be awake when the real thing happens, so she comes."

We get in the car and Mom takes a scarf out of her pocket. "Now I am going to blindfold you. No peeking, promise!" I pull it down around my neck. I think of Patty Hearst. I wonder how long you can breathe in the trunk of a Volkswagen. I do know that they're supposed to float like boats in the water if the windows stay shut. I think of the woman in our apartment complex who drove her brand-new Cadillac Deville into the swamp to die. The two boys who saw her and leapt in to rescue her said she was in the car, just floating there. When she saw them, she popped the trunk with a fancy button inside the glove compartment and the swamp sucked her in backward as fast as a snapping turtle snagging a duck. I push these thoughts aside. Mom wants to train me, not kill me.

"Here's the deal, Gingie. You just don't know how any of this is going to happen, pumpkin. When the war starts, someone could be taking you out to see the children, someone who has to keep their arrival point a secret even from you. There could also be a kidnapping. Someone who takes you away because they don't want you to help the war children. The thing is: You never know who's who. That's why we never talk to anyone about the secret war. That's why you have to always pay attention." She pulls the scarf back over my eyes.

I close my eyes under the blindfold and lay out a map in my head. Mom starts the car. I know that my starting point is our driveway and I pay attention to the turns the car makes, trying not to anticipate where we're going, but making a list in my head. Left turn out of driveway, right turn soon after. We seem to drift to the left, I hear gravel and sand, then we turn around, back onto the street to the right. Then another left. Uphill a bit, gear shift, turnaround. We stop. Mom helps me out of the car. Frogs and cicadas. Off the road. Scrub grass and weeds against the legs of my jeans. Down a hill and then we're next to the water. Low tide and the marsh smells oily and alive.

Mom has her hand on my shoulder and walks behind me. For a long time it's just the scruff of sea grass under my shoes. We're in the woods. The air is cool on my face and then I can smell the pine needles. We stop and I hear Mom rustle through her pack. "Your job is to get back to the duck blind. I'll be waiting for you there." She lights a match for her cigarette—a hiss and then the sharp sulfur smell. Her hand is

back on my shoulder and we keep walking. I have to keep re-
minding myself to come back to the list in my head. To focus
on this one thing. My mind wanders. I can't stop thinking
about the coats we bought for the war children. There's one
with a bit of rabbit fur at the collar. When Mom is out I plan
on hiding it. I'll snip off its soft collar and put it under my pillow or in my pocket to carry with me. I love the feel of it,
warm and soft and somehow alive. I want a whole blanket
made of fur to wrap myself in, but I want the fur on the inside, next to my skin. There's an old book on the shelves that
tells me how to trap and skin rabbits and I will save enough
pelts and stitch them together and wrap myself in all that
warm soft fur. In a blanket like that I would never be cold. A
blanket like that would hold only the best dreams.

Mom's gone. I realize it just like that. There is no hand on my
shoulder, no one pushing me forward, just my own movement. I pull the blindfold down around my neck and wait for
my eyes to adjust. The pines look icy with the moon on the
needles. Everything looks sharp and clear and clean. And
empty.

From *How to Survive in the Woods* I remember that the best way
to look for tracks is to look for something irregular in the
landscape. Pine needles have fallen here for years. Animals
come through. Deer and dogs. Birds. Once I start looking it's
easy enough to see the line of our path. I shuffled my feet all
the way. I should remember to do that when the war really
happens. I follow the trail to the road. Mom's dropped me off
at the end of Beach Road—home is a straight shot half mile
walk. I don't see one car the whole way back, though the
Moores' collie comes out to inspect me. I stop at the cottage

to get a glass of milk before I go to the duck blind. Mom's stretched out on the sofa. "The mosquitoes are awful out there," she yawns. "What time is it?"

"Four-thirty."

"Not bad for your first time."

"Thanks." I say. I'm pleased to have passed my first test.

"Sit down with me?"

I sit beside her on the sofa and she strokes my hair. "I love you," she croons. "I'd kill for you. You're mine."

I know she loves me, no matter what.

2000

*W*here were you those early months we were down at the cottage?" I ask my father when I interview him on the phone. "What were you thinking?"

"I was in Virginia Beach. Working." His voice halts.

I don't budge, I refuse to fill the silence he has left on the other end of the line. Even at thirty-three I am as furious as a child who thinks she's been forsaken.

"I don't know what to tell you. I don't know what I thought. Things were so bad and your mother loved Kechotan. I thought maybe it might be the one thing that would help her. Of course," he says dryly, "that wasn't the case."

Over the years it's been easy for me to lose track of the fact of my father's loss of my mother. He loved her too.

Now I can't speak. Even though he's agreed to be interviewed, I can't find my way through the questions on my list. They all start to sound like one small cry of why, why, why,

didn't you do something, and I am ashamed of my wretchedness, my neediness, all these long years later.

I decide to be more direct: "What did you think when you
saw Mom had painted the windows black?"

The silence again and I grip the edge of the kitchen table to
stop my hand from shaking.

"That's so funny," he says. "Until you just mentioned it, I'd
completely forgotten that she did that."

Is this a joke? No. Is he lying? No. Is my father's spotty
memory really spotty? No. Nor has his memory been erased
by trauma. The fact of the matter is simple. He wasn't there
for much of the time the windows were black. When he finally did agree to live with us at the cottage, he fought with
my mother, scraped the windows clean and was done with it.

During that time we are all isolated: my mother by her
madness, my father and me by our distance, my sister by her
age. And so the next question is mine to answer. I wonder: Is
there a collective meaning, an understanding of those years
that we can share through our separate memories?

2000

*M*y father and sister are helpful as I research back in our history. But I spent most of my time at the cottage in those days with my mother and I wonder what she recalls. I decide I will write my mother and ask her what she remembers. She responds with three letters in as many weeks.

Dear Virginia,

Thanks for the letter. About the field hospital. I needed to put the cottage in a state of readiness. When I came home with you and Emma I got to see my father in Newport News and he pointed out certain things we would be needing. 1. A fire extinguisher. 2. A microwave oven for different things to be sterilized. Now the table was sturdy enough to be a hospital examination table for surgery and other things. Like getting under it with planes passing over.

I was to do this in silence.

Your dad helped me fix up the cottage for the hospital without knowing it. Now everything looked beautiful. Now it's combat-ready for us in case of attack.

You see, the cottage is hidden from crossing planes from Langley. So there are secrets you keep for your safety. My father and I decided on a space heater that we should have for heat and your father got a hot plate and we could cook on the top, soup or warm rolls or whatever. Your father built shelves and painted walls that could be washed. Now that is complete.

Also my father had the trees trimmed to be safe from falling limbs and trees growing over the wires connected to the house. He also told me we were safer than most because of the way the cottage was situated.

You see there we are hidden from the major attack people. We are surrounded by the Coast Guard, Camp Perry, Fort Eustis, the shipyard, the Navy, and the oil refinery. More than likely they would be attacked but the way Chuck's house is and Pearline's, and the other houses are exposed. Ours is hidden. Our roof looks like pine needles. Lisa and Chuck are exposed to air traffic—we have the safest place. Hidden. My father said if you want to live, stay at the cottage.

I saved all the plastic bottles for plasma.

Margaret came for a visit and she gave us the Red Cross book to learn what was in there.

So I read and tried to see what to do in case of emergency.

Our friend Tom came down, he was a doctor, and visited. I still need to move the bathroom to the room that you and Emma used to sleep in. And turn the table. Tom was going to be a surgeon, which should be done by now. I never got around to it.

So in a sense it was an adventure doing all that but I wanted to be ready for attack. You see the cottage is on the border of the United States. We are so close to the water in case of fire, which is good. Well, we do at least have a safe home away from a fire attack so I need to get down there and move the bathroom and open up the kitchen. We are mighty lucky.

I've got to go to dinner now, so much love to you all.
Mom

Dear Virginia,

Sorry I took so long answering your letter.

You asked what you did during the years at the cottage. Your favorite friend was *Carol Carpenter.* You usually could be found at the *Carpenters'* or Miss Ruth's. She was a retired schoolteacher. She was married late in life. She loved you and Emma too.

I worked at the Newport News Shipyard as Ed Campbell's personnel director. I made an excellent salary—$68,762. I gave my money to Chuck and Lisa to hold for me. So they have my money with them. I had to make a plane ticket to go to France to investigate using drugs used on shipyard employees. I took Darby with me. These pills they were pushing are the same as the pills the doctors give me.

When we first lived down at the cottage we went crabbing on the sandbars. Your major problem when you went to Kechotan Elementary was finding your shoes every day in time for the bus. I thought I'd lose my mind hunting shoes down before the school bus got there, but somehow you got there in time.

My friend Warren was in a POW camp. To rescue him I had to go to flight school. After I finally passed flight school we took off for Alaska. I drove the plane and landed and got the POWs out of prison. I flew around the world in a sleet storm. I landed the jet at Langley. People there were running all around. I never will forget landing that plane and holding you in my thoughts. I praye d, Dear Father, I'll never leave my child, even when she leaves me.

Walter is in another POW camp. I don't know where he is, but he told me he would find me and never leave me alone in such a turmoil.

My finger is beginning to hurt so will stop. Anyway in general, that is what took place.

> My love to you.
> Mom

Dear Gingie:

Back to you and Carol. I was cooking supper and just having a laughing fit at you and Carol outside the window stark naked playing with the hose. All of a sudden I heard laughter and there you were having a ball.

Emma and I usually went to the cove and played with the sand fiddler crabs and little things. She loved that and decided she was going to be a zoologist.

Sunday evenings I flew you and Emma out to a small island

where the blood was being stored in case of a fire. The moon looked beautiful coming across the bay for the landing. It was quite an experience. We did our part and got our blood there.

We lived quite the life there.

David Brinkley became our friend and took us to Connecticut. One night I found him outside our door begging for help. He stayed with us for a while and then went shopping and bought you clothes and me too.

That is all I remember, so come to see me when you can.

Love,
   Mom

For days after I got these letters I tried to pick the truth from the delusion. But it made me frustrated, angry and wild inside.

"How can I make any sense of this!" I cried to my husband. I wanted him to tell me that no one could ever make sense of nonsense. To stop this immensely futile effort.

Instead he looked at me and said kindly, "How on earth did you manage this when you were a child?"

1975

*E*very morning before Mom wakes I am to learn a chapter in the *Complete First Aid Manual*. When she gets up she usually quizzes me while I fix her coffee. Of course, this is Mom's idea. She is convinced at some point during the war we will be separated—I'll need to know how to take care of myself and the children.

I like to imagine the war children arriving at night, feeling their way to the cottage by the moss on the trees, like we're part of some underground railroad. The children will be silent and shocked and even when their mouths open to weep, they will make no sound. They won't flinch as I root and dig the thorns from their feet. I'll wrap them in blankets that I'll warm on a line by the fire and give them Creomulsion to quiet their coughs.

My favorite chapter is poisonous snakebites. I see myself unafraid, tearing tourniquets from my skirt, heating the blade of a knife and slicing the deep punctures, sucking and spitting the sour blood until my mouth and lips tingle, swollen from the venom.

Today is compound fractures. The blue-and-gray illustrations show arms and legs jointed and dangling at strange angles. Jagged bones cut through the skin. I wonder how much blood there would be. Two people are needed sometimes to wrench the bones back inside so they can set. You need antibiotics. Sometimes surgery. There's a section on gangrene, but it makes me sweat, and I turn the book over. Then I sneak out. My cousins are gone on vacation to Pennsylvania. So I go and knock on the door of Ruth Smith's house. Miss Ruth is always home and always busy. I try to visit when it is time for lunch—she makes the best lemon pound cake in the world.

Miss Ruth sticks her head from around the side of her garage. "Over here, girl!" She gives me a small basket to gather plums for her to can this weekend.

"Careful, now," Miss Ruth warns as I balance in the fork of her plum tree. "I don't need you to fall."

I reach up with one hand and hold the small basket with my other. My toes curl and grip the slick limbs.

"By the stems, girl! Don't smudge them up."

I pinch the stems from the tree and lower the plums one by one into the basket, careful not to disturb their powdery surface.

"Get a few leaves, too. Ooh, damsons look so pretty with that icy bloom. I'll put them in Grandma Smith's crystal fruit dish and set it on the dining room table. I just can't bear to put up damson preserves right away."

I bend down and put the basket into Miss Ruth's hands and then jump out of the tree.

"Little daredevil. You get that from your grandma." She takes a bite out of one of the damsons and the juice trickles down her chin. "Sweet." She hands me the rest of the plum and I put it whole in my mouth, sucking until there is only pit. I toss it in the ditch. Miss Ruth's sky blue eyes catch me and then disappear in the shadow of her hat. "Plenty of likeness beyond the name."

"I like Gingie, not Virginia."

"Well, that's simply awful, I think. Grinchie!"

"Gingie."

Miss Ruth flaps her hands at me. "Grinchie. Ginger. I'll call you Virginia. You do remind me of her."

I don't think I look like her. "I've seen pictures," I say. "She was fat."

"Oh, you've got a bit of her around the eyes. I'm talking your spirit. That's passed down too.

"Take my boy," she sighs. "Never really knew his pap. Killed long before a child can remember things." She walks over to the airplane propellers that are knifed into the ground on either side of her drive. They've been painted white so many times you can see the outlines of different levels of chipped paint, marking years like rings in a tree. "But he got Henry's itchy feet. That boy can't stay put. Just went to Brazil and brought me back the prettiest amethysts you've ever seen. Cut them out of the side of a mountain himself."

"Did Mr. Henry die in a war?"

"No. Made it through Okinawa and Korea without a scratch. He'd dust for bugs in the summers for the little extra. Plane just stopped running and he fell right out of the sky. Those little planes aren't much." She pats the propeller.

I try to think of something to say to her, but I'm sorry is the best I come up with.

She smiles when I say it. "He was such a sweet boy. Brought me flowers every Friday. Always smelled good, too." Her hat falls to her back and she molds her white curls between her hands and sighs.

"Your pap, where's he?"

"Virginia Beach."

"Doesn't he want to be with you and Molly?"

I sigh back at her. "He has to work. School starts in ten days." My voice sounds like it belongs to someone else. "He'll be down to take us back." I hear words rise and crack, like I'm telling a lie.

"None of my business, dear."

"No—" I say and my voice squeezes shut.

"I need to check on that rump roast," she says and flutters up the back path.

I take my time and get myself together. This is what I know: My father will come down, I know him. I also know that before Lisa and Chuck took the girls to Pennsylvania for two weeks, she filled out a registration form for me for school, just in case. She even called Dr. Kirschmeier to get my vaccinations. So there's a small chance that I might be here for ome school. What does Ruth Smith know about it anyway? Old widow woman living alone in this house for practically ever.

I think about just walking off and leaving her and her big fat rump roast, but she didn't mean anything. Besides, where would I go? I'm tired of spending time alone; there's nothing to do. Even the freshly dead muskrat that I'd poked with a stick in the ditch three days ago was now just paper-thin bones turning to jelly. There's nothing else to do besides visit Miss Ruth.

Ashes comes over and rubs his face against my ankles, licks the back of my knee with his tail. "Hey, cat." He cocks his head to have each ear scratched and then springs all mouth and claws on a blue skink. The bloody tail cringes in his mouth and he gnashes at it with his little brown teeth until it stills. I follow him up the path to the back door. He drops it on the stoop, twists one paw under the screen door, and lets himself in.

Miss Ruth is weighing her portion of cut potatoes. "I shouldn't eat these at all, doctor says potato starch'll send my sugar up fast. But I can't resist."

She sets two pots of potatoes on the stove to boil and then pats the scale. Ashes jumps into the cradle and sits. "Twenty-one pounds! You're getting to be such a fat old Tom." The white metal scale clatters as Ashes jumps to the floor before she can swat him. He scratches at the pantry door and twitches his back.

"No more food for you till supper." She holds the screen door open and he walks out to the stoop. "Now go find a girl-friend and work up an appetite." He rubs his whiskers on the warm granite steps and rolls over, all white belly. "Lazy thing." She hooks the door against him.

Her kitchen is an immaculate yellow and white. The air from the window blows through the smells of roast, boiled tea, and burnt sugar. There's another smell under it all that has seeped into the house, the smell of Miss Ruth herself, heavy and soft, like earth. It's a cool comforting odor, and every time I'm in her house I want to sleep, I feel that safe.

"Were you and my grandmother friends?"

"We graduated high school together in 1926. There were seven girls and six boys in our class. Too small a class not to be friends. We girls did everything together." Her face is damp from heat; a wet curl pressed against her cheek is turning orange from her powder. She pats her neck with a dish towel. "She was something else, your grandmother."

"Was she like Mom?"

"Lord, no!" she snorts and starts to wave her hand, but it stops midair and she smoothes it along the edge of her apron.

My lips feel numb and dry.

"You don't remember her, do you?"

"She died before I was born, makes it kind of hard." I'm surprised at my smart mouth.

Miss Ruth clicks her tongue and blows out a breath. "I suppose she did."

"Sometimes I don't like Mom much either." There, I think, I've said it.

Miss Ruth taps the end of a steaming metal spoon against my chest. "Don't you let me hear those words cross your lips again. Your mother loves you. She'd die before she'd let anything happen to you. For shame!"

I open my eyes wide to hold back their water. No one will see me cry.

"Go get the napkins and silver from the buffet."

I push through the swinging door into the parlor. The drapes are drawn against the heat and it takes a minute for my eyes to adjust to the dark room. The smell of Miss Ruth is deepest in here. She spends most of her days sitting on the red velvet sofa crocheting. On the table, on top of a stack of *People* magazines, is a large cardboard circle covered in wax paper. Her starched Christmas stars are pinned down to dry—they're stretched tight, like captured butterflies. She uses a needle the size of a toothpick and makes them while she watches Lawrence Welk. I never see her look down except during a commercial, when she'll pick up the large magnifying glass on the table and inspect her work.

I pull the pins out of the smallest damp star and fold it into my pocket. Then I go over to the buffet, open the small mahogany silver box, and gather our silver together for dinner. The utensils clatter dully as I set a fistful down on the dark polished top. The brass knobs on the small drawers of the buffet don't make a sound as I lift them. But I can't make myself pull forward to open them. My hands burn. Nothing I can take from Miss Ruth will stop this feeling. She would give me anything I asked for. But the thought of asking, of opening my mouth and speaking, makes me feel dizzy and sick. I stand up and press my hands against the top of the buffet to steady myself. To make sure I don't take anything else. Unwrapped peppermints sit on a crystal dish at the end of the buffet. They smell sharp and sticky and I can feel one in my mouth.

"Dinner's almost done," she calls through the door.

I hear the ice snap in our glasses as she pours tea.

"I will not steal from Miss Ruth," I whisper.

The door opens and swings three times before it shuts. I don't move. Miss Ruth walks up behind me and I hear her untie her apron.

"Take a peppermint."

I lift my hands from the wood. Their shape is outlined in steamy prints that shrink inward to the palm and then vanish.

"No," I say and then turn around to look at her face. I meet her blue eyes and immediately I feel cool and clear and empty. "I don't need it."

2000

I needed to steal, but never from stores or strangers. When I stole, it was from people I knew. Even people I loved. From my aunt I took little bottles of perfume and seashells she'd collected; from my cousins, I stole pens, lipsticks, and candy money. From my uncle, beautiful fishing lures that looked like alien jewelry and arrowheads he'd found. Years later, I stole from all the women whose children I babysat. Earrings, perfume, once several packs of birth control pills that I ground up and fed to my indoor plants (I'd read it made them grow). I reasoned these people had so much they would never miss what I took, though surely they knew.

I was aware early on that people were afraid of my mother and, worse, afraid of their feelings of pity and disgust. It didn't take long for a smart kid to figure out that their fear translated into a certain amount of power. I could get away with things that my peers never could. Adults turned a blind eye. I told myself at the time that my thieving was an act of meanness, a way of taking what I wanted from people who had more than they needed. (A clever trick to appoint oneself both Robin Hood and the poor—but if Patty/Tania and most of the SLA could pull it off, why not me?) But it was simpler than that: I wanted to be them. I longed to lead a life filled with good smells and pretty things and well-ordered closets. The lives of the people I stole from looked so easy. And as a child it never occurred to me that such lives could be earned. I figured life was something that was forced upon you and that you endured. Like my mother, or the lack of her.

1975

*M*y mother begins keeping notebooks, enormous five-subject spiral-bound books where she records the progress of the secret war. She makes no effort to conceal her jottings. I sneak a look, but her notes are about as interesting as reading someone's old grocery list. What's exciting is that Mom is always "on guard." We are always to be on the lookout for clues. Like the color red that was one of my mother's first signals about the secret war, clues come to us by ingenious means. They can be broadcast to her telepathically via the CIA or they can appear in the environment. Many clues Mom finds in magazines or books. What she sees, how she reaches her conclusions as to what's a clue and what isn't, she never reveals. Soon she has gathered so many clues that she says it is important to lay them all out and try to assemble them, like pieces of a puzzle. She does this by creating art. She takes art books and pictures from magazines along with the things we have gathered on our walks and glues them to nearly every surface in the house. Our bedroom doors, the walls, the toilet lid and seat cover, the edges of the bathroom mirror, even the the old Kenmore refrigerator with the pull handle and tiny frost-encrusted freezer box not big enough to hold a half gallon of ice cream is transformed into an assemblage of personal history and current events. The refrigerator is the masterpiece—the first picture that catches your eye is of Dick and Pat Nixon, smiling, in the upper right-hand corner. There are pictures of family, strange quotes my mother has written and then antiqued by burning the edges with a match flame. On the bottom of the refrigerator is the paperback cover of *Jude the Obscure*, which shows Jude's face fractured like stained-glass shards and pictures of his children hung by their necks in the background. I look for any occasion to spill something on this image until finally the corner of the cover comes away and I tear it off and bury it, terrified of the consequences. But my mother doesn't notice.

Clues also come in other forms. And I discover the thing that every treasure hunter or private eye must know, that once you have a bit of code, a sign, a clue, it is impossible to stop looking for more. It's addictive. The world as you know it ceases to exist and is replaced with a universe bottomless with intrigue. The simplest exchange can become an opportunity to uncover more information and crack the case. For me, it is like being Nancy Drew, without the red sports car, or any real case to crack. But who cares? It is the thrill of the thing, not the solution of the mystery that is interesting.

Mother, Emma, and I take long walks through the marsh looking for signs. Mother picks up a dull aluminum can and tosses it back down, but a piece of yellow nylon rope tangled in a blackberry bush means something. As does a washed-up piece of a buoy. I run through the sea grass, bringing her fragments of things to pass judgment on. An old medicine bottle, a boiled crab shell, a moldly cornhusk doll. What do these things mean? Sometimes she brings a clue home with us to study, as she did the day we found a half-rotted duck decoy. But usually she just nods, shows her approval, or shakes her head. Mom records everything in her notebooks as we go to sleep at night.

1975

September comes and my father is still stationed primarily in Virginia Beach. He comes down on weekends and some weeknights and now seems to get the fact that my mother is not going to move us back. So, with no good-byes to friends in Virginia Beach and no great preparation, I begin fourth grade in Kechotan. Just before school starts I convince myself that I can start my life all over. That I can say anything and be anyone I want to. I can tell the kids I am from Alaska. Or that my parents are archaeologists and that I am in Kechotan on a quest for a lost pirate ship. Finally, I settle on telling people that my mother and I are artists—painters.

The first day of school I splatter bright paint on my jeans and tie one of mother's bandannas over my head. I even try piercing my own ears with a darning needle, but it hurts so much I quit without even drawing blood.

My plans to embellish my history are soon thwarted. Kechotan is a small town; everyone knows everybody else and their families. Since the kids have all been in school together since first grade, the arrival of a new student is a major event. My two older cousins are only too happy for the attention that comes from having more information about me than anyone else. People soon know about me too, and a little bit about my mother, and where I am living.

Soon I dread school each day and find it pure misery except for Carol Carpenter, an outgoing girl with trusty brown eyes and a head full of lush tumbled curls.

I am smitten with Carol the first time I see her and I believe that if I can make her my friend, then no one at school will ever bother me again and that somehow, I will stand in a sliver of the light that shines from her.

Carol says hello to me each day and even bothers to tell me she likes my lunchbox or notebook. Carol is unlike anyone else in Kechotan. Her manner of dress is sporty, yet girlish. She favors simple skirts or plaid bell-bottom pants and peter pan–collared shirts with colorful piping. She has pierced ears and wears chunky gold hoop earrings that, along with her clogs and her downy blonde upper lip, give her a vague gypsy look that makes her simultaneously mysterious and approachable. I think of her as a gypsy Girl Scout. Carol never wears Fleetwood Mac T-shirts or pastel T's with sparkly silk-screened unicorns or Hobbit-inspired wizards that look like they belong on the side of someone's super-cool van.

Carol hangs out with Vicki Harrison, the coolest, yet most outcast girl in the fourth grade class. Vicki was put back a year because her test scores were so low. She says when those test were passed out, she just filled in the holes with her number-two pencil any way she pleased.

Since Carol likes Vicki, I know that there is hope for me. It's clear that Carol's true love is strays. Vicki's five-foot-seven height and long pendulous breasts make her look as if she belongs in tenth grade, not fourth. The braver boys tease her, but most people are scared and awed by her. Vicki tries to make the girls feel better about the fact that our breasts have not even begun to sprout by telling us "how they get in the way of everything" and make her back ache. Vicki has long, oily brown hair that she curling-irons away from her face in two long tubes; mean-looking acne shines from her chin and brow; and she wears a thick cowhide bracelet she made in shop class that stamps out her name. The absolute coolest thing about Vicki is that she recently purchased a massive leather purse from Lerner's, which all the girls suspect means one thing—period. Vicki is way ahead of the curve; the film on menstruation isn't even shown till the sixth grade.

*   *   *

One afternoon in PE class, we're sitting outside on the cracked tennis courts, waiting our turn to claim a racket and bat a ball across the net. Melinda Murphy is sitting by us. She is a small pale girl who recently turned up with scabs erupting all over her legs. She is clearly poor and is usually unkempt and smells like curdled milk. Her mother, folks say, is dying in a hospital in Fairfield, but I didn't know for sure what the truth was. Her family lives in the absolute worst part of Messick, and her house is practically next door to the dump.

But nothing keeps Melinda from speaking up in class and her grades are almost always A's and B's. She must know that most everyone is repulsed by her or pities her or both, but she doesn't react to people's teasing or their ignoring her. Still, I always steer clear of Melinda. I know my smirched social standing at school will be reduced to dust if I get too near her. I never would have dreamt of even speaking a word to her but Carol goes and invites her over to sit with us.

Before you know it she is telling us a story of how her brother Peter had taken a poop in the outhouse and how he looked at his turd and saw it crawling with worms. I feel my body stiffen. I'd had pinworms the summer before and the doctor had given me some medicine for it—my mother had been wildly upset over the little white worms writhing in my stools but I wasn't about to say any of that to Melinda. Her family didn't go to the doctor's unless there was a true emergency. Her father dabs gasoline on her scabby legs to cure them, she says, just the same as he did for their dogs' mange.

"That's happened to me too!" Carol says of the pinworms and Melinda leans in and asks what it is you have to do for it. Carol tells her there are pills you take that kill the worms and the itty-bitty eggs inside your intestines. Melinda nods and looks hard at a thorny-leaved dandelion poking through the chain-link fence. Oh, she says coolly, then yanks the dandelion flower through the fence and loops the stem like a little loose knot beneath it. "Hey, look, Mama had a baby and its head popped off!" she sings and as she tightens the knot the flower snaps free and zings off Vicki's forehead.

"You know I might have some leftover pills at home," Carol says. In case the first dose doesn't get them all. "I'll bring in what's left."

This is the sort of thing that makes me love Carol and want

to be just like her. She isn't ever ashamed of who she is and she isn't ashamed of who you are.

Right then Carol looks at Vicki's purse and asks her if she has her period. Vicki nods and smiles, obviously pleased to share her secret. "I tried putting a Tampax in but it about killed me. It was like being stabbed and Mama said it might break my maidenhead."

I have no idea what on earth a maidenhead is or even when you get one, but it sounds both important and awful. Then Vicki pulls out an enormous Kotex pad and sets it before us. My mother wears tampons and I have never seen a pad close up before. It smells sweet, like talcum powder, and gleams big and white as a fish in the sun. All of us regard the pad with awe and a fierce jealousy. "Can I borrow it?" Melinda asks.

"Do you need one?" Vicki says and we watch as Melinda considers lying and then shakes her head. "Naw. I just wanted to have one for my purse—y'know, in case."

Vicki picks up the pad and places it back into the secret zippered compartment inside her purse. "I would lend it to you, but I flood a lot the first couple of days. I might need it. Sorry." Right then I don't know whether I will die of embarrassment or jealousy. I am supposed to be Carol's best friend. I won't be pushed aside by the likes of Vicki and Melinda.

*   *   *

Life with Mom and the secret war made me a keen listener and observer. In short order I discover that Carol Carpenter is the only Baptist among a homeroom full of Methodists (excepting Marcella and Marcia Capelletti, twin sisters who were allowed to be Catholic since their father who worked at Langley, had moved them here from Palermo, Italy.

When Dad comes to the cottage that weekend, I grill him for answers about religion. I have never spent one second in a church in my life but I am a quick study. My father explains that he was raised as an Episcopalian, and though his family had rarely attended services, he nonetheless knows all the hymns by heart by from his days at St. Bartholomew's Academy, a boys' school in Fairfield. Now he says he is atheist.

When I ask my mother she says she was raised Baptist, but now says she is agnostic. To declare herself an atheist, she says, well, that would be "tacky and extreme, like Jane Fonda sympathizing with the Communists." Besides, Mom whispers to me that the Communists are atheists and that she, well, she is an All-American patriot indeed—her recruitment into the secret war proves that. At this, my father leaves the house to take a walk outside.

1975

*B*y the end of the weekends I long for school, for anyplace that isn't with my mother. The kids now leave me alone, so it's bearable. Even Miss Alexander has quit bothering me. She goes up and down each row calling out questions but skips over me every time, so I just spend my mornings staring out the window.

I imagine that I am Ashes, Miss Ruth's cat, curled up on a sunny spot of carpet. The little hairs on my face rise and itch from the dazzle of white reflected from my paper. All morning I stare outside until the light has bleached my vision and my view is dull and gray. A man with a cane blurs and hovers on the sidewalk. My ears fill with a sound like the tense roar of the surf. I put my head on my desk, my nose buried in the salty nook of my elbow and breathe until I am almost asleep, dreaming that I was floating on the warm salt water.

"Gingie. Gingie. Time for lunch." Marcella Capelletti jabs at my arm with her pencil eraser. "Get up, get up!" she whispers. I raise my head and the room tilts and rocks. My face feels numb. When I stand I can't seem to steady myself. I tremble and my teeth chatter in my head and the sound they make makes me chatter even more. Miss Alexander comes over, presses one dry cool hand against my forehead, and then wipes it on her pants leg. "Walk her to the clinic, Marcella. She's burning up."

In the clinic my ears burn and itch deep inside my head. Mrs. Williams, the substitute nurse, takes me out of my coat and seats me on the wooden bench. The clinic is cool and dim. The walls are a green-painted cinderblock and the lights are all off except for a little brass lamp on her desk. She puts a thermometer under my tongue and my teeth clatter against the glass so much that I'm afraid I'll break the thing and wind up with a mouthful of mercury. "Stick your thumb in your mouth. Like this." She jams her thumb between her back teeth. I feel like a baby when I do it, but it works. Mrs. Williams takes my pulse while I stare at her shimmery white thumbnail. Then she tucks my hair behind my right ear and peers inside with a little black cone. The touch of her hand and fingernails on my face feels so gentle and sure that my mouth falls open and my eyes sting and fill with water. I wish I could throw myself in her neck and cry. I wonder if maybe she gave a baby up for adoption years ago and that I am really her child.

"Does that hurt?" she asks. I close my eyes and shake my head. She repeats the examination on my left ear. I am put on a cot with a clean white sheet and white blanket. "Just an ear infection, child." She presses a cold washcloth on my forehead. "Doctor'll give you some penicillin and it'll clear right up. You rest." I lean my face against the cinderblock wall and listen to the slow dial of the phone. A girl from my class drops off my book bag and leaves it on the bench.

"There's no answer at your aunt's so I'm going to drive you home myself."

Stretched out in the back of Mrs. Williams's car, I realize that no one except the kids who ride our bus know where I live. I can tell by the perfect blue vinyl seats in Mrs. Williams's sedan that she has a big sunny house that she keeps as free of dust as she does the metal-topped glass jars full of cotton in the school clinic. I imagine she walks around her house never dirtying her white pantsuit.

"Our house, it's at the end of Hunt's Neck Road," I tell her. "But you can drop me off at the end of the driveway."

"Lie back down in that seat. Drop you off. Good night. There are procedures. I have to get your mother to sign this paper saying I returned you safely home."

"Mom doesn't like to sign papers. I'm feeling better; the fresh air would do me good."

Mrs. Williams glances in the rearview mirror then takes a hard look at her fingernails. "I've worked as school nurse for ten years, girl. Yours isn't the only poor family in Kechotan. No shame in it certainly. There's worse." A blast of heat scalds my face. Suddenly, I understand what everyone except me thinks: I am poor. But we're not poor. We just live here. We're preparing for a war. I think about telling Mrs. Williams. She's a nurse. Maybe she could be of use. But I am stunned. Everyone believes I am poor.

Worse than being poor, of course, is being lazy and dirty, and when Mom comes to the door wrapped in her blanket and squinting at the light I see old ashes flaking on the blanket and a splotch of ketchup on her chin. Emma is on the sofa watching *The Electric Company* on the black-and-white Dad has brought down.

"Mrs. Roberts, I'm Sue Williams, the school nurse. We tried contacting you through your sister-in-law, but there was no answer. Looks like Gingie's got an ear infection. Both ears, I'd say."

Mom pulls her hair behind her ears and licks her lips. "I see."

Mrs. Williams waited for Mom to say something else and then she took a slow step back like she just spied a sleepy copperhead. At first I thought she was scared of Mom, but she was looking hard at the windows.

"She needs to see a doctor," she says, still staring at the cottage. "He'll put her on a course of penicillin to clear it up. I'll go ahead and make an appointment with Dr. Nicholas for this afternoon."

"That's quite all right. The family doctor is Smith, in Newport News. I can make arrangements myself. Thank you for bringing her home."

Mrs. Williams reaches into her purse and pulls out a crisp white envelope. "I need you to sign this release saying that Gingie was returned home in satisfactory condition."

"Except for the ear infection," Mother says and then writes *returned with both ears infected* on the bottom of the page and signs the paper against the door frame.

"Feeling a bit under the weather yourself?" Mrs. Williams asks as Mother starts to close the door.

"Not a bit," Mother smiles. "Good day." She closes the door fast before Mrs. Williams can say anything else.

Mother immediately unbuttons my coat, hangs it over the back of the chair, and slips a hand under my shirt. "The fever's in your belly." She goes into the bathroom and runs the shower until the room is white with steam. "Give me your clothes and stay in until the hot water runs out." The noise of the water makes me dizzy. I sit on the shower floor and watch the water slide off my body, leaving behind hundreds of perfect shiny beads that balance among the dark hairs on my legs.

When the water runs cold, I step out in the fog. Mother is waiting for me with a fresh towel. She wraps it around me twice, sets me on the commode, and towels off my hair. She brings her flannel nightgown for me to wear and a pair of new white socks from the war children's supply. She rolls the sleeves up so my fingers are exposed, but I curl them back under the cuffs liking the too-big feeling. With a quick slice of the comb she parts my hair on the wrong side and then opens the door.

"Hop in bed."

The room seems as foggy as the bathroom, but then I realize that it's smoke.

"You made a fire."

"A little one, there was some old wood in the shed. Once the damp burns out the smoke'll disappear."

"I don't mind. Smells good."

My bed is made with new sheets and blankets from the

supplies. Mother has even put her extra pillow on the bed to prop me up. I slide under the heavy blankets. Finally I am warm and sleepy.

I close my eyes and smell the pine smoke and hear Mother at the stove. A metal spoon scrapes against a metal pot. Stirring soup. She brings over a small cream pitcher.

"Take the pillows out from behind your head, Gingie."

"What's that?"

"A little warm paraffin from Aunt Lisa's preserves. It'll make your ears feel better."

I put my head on the sheet and turn one ear up. Then mother pours in the wax. For a second the itching and burning in my ears is worse and then the thick heat fills every inside ache. She tells me to lie still until the liquid sets and then pours the rest of the blackberry-smelling wax into my other ear.

When she's done the sounds in the cottage became as dim as the light. "I can't hear very well," I say. And even to myself my voice is muted and cottony.

"Use your other senses. Sometimes I imagine I'm deaf and turn the television volume down to practice reading lips. It may come in handy. You just use your eyes in a different way."

"Am I going to be deaf?" I ask, imagining myself learning that secret language of hands and fingers.

"I don't think so. Not from this."

"Oh."

Mom pulls the big armchair next to my bed and spreads an afghan across her lap.

"It's kind of nice with you home, sick. I miss you when you're at school."

I act like I am asleep.

"You know when I was little we used to live in Savannah. In those days my hair wasn't black, it was white from the sun. We lived in a little house at the very end of a dead-end street. Out beyond our fence was the giant parking lot for the drive-in movie. Chuck and I would climb up onto the fence after supper and watch the shows until it was time for bed. Since we didn't have a little speaker, all the pictures were silent, but it was easy enough to figure out what was being said. My favorite was *Samson and Delilah*. Oh, I watched that film every night it was at the drive-in. It was so exciting. I begged my mother to take me to the theater in town so I could really see the show. She thought the picture shows were tacky. But finally I convinced her that it was *Samson and Delilah*; it was the Bible, for chrissakes. And one Saturday afternoon we dressed up and went to the matinee in town. I was thrilled. The music was wonderful. I finally got to hear Hedy Lamarr's voice. But no, I wasn't prepared for what they did to Samson. Even though I'd seen the part where they burn his eyes out with hot coals, I hadn't heard his screams. And when Samson screamed, I screamed too. I was so hysterical my mother took me from the theater with my hands flat against my ears. So, see, it's not always such a great thing to have all your senses working at the same time."

I slide my hand in between my mattress and boxspring and get the little crocheted star I stole from Miss Ruth. I slip my hand into my pillowcase so I can hold it in secret. I think of it as my guide star, my North Star. I hold it with my fingers. Then I go still and breathe just loud enough for her to think she's put me to sleep. I think maybe Mom's right. Maybe this wax in my ears will be enough to block out her voice. Then when she starts in on me all I will have to do is close my eyes and she'll be gone. My fingers will have the softness of her gown, my body, the warm bed. My nose and tongue the sharp pine smoke of the fire. I think that maybe being deaf or blind is like being magic. You can make people disappear and then drop the curtain before anyone can think to ask How.

1975

I am reading John Steinbeck's *The Pearl*, which has been on display in the library. It's a good story and one rainy September afternoon, reading it in bed, my mother becomes focused on it. When she becomes fixed on something, her demeanor changes. She gets a look in her eye that widens as if someone has just told her the worst secret, and then, it seems, her face tilts back and she fills with a strange energy. The easiest course of action is to just let my mother have at it until it is past. To confront her, to obstruct her path, her destined vision, which is always right, no matter what, is to lose big time. It is always to lose.

I know immediately that my book is doomed. So when Mother takes the book away from me, I stand still and watch as she sets out to destroy it. "I can't believe that they would let you have this shit. What sort of pornography is this? Look at this." There is a watercolor of a woman with brown bare breasts on the front, but my mother isn't reacting to the nudity, though it may have been what first caught her eye. My mother isn't uptight—she is pasted nudes on the refrigerator and had hung a nude in our bathroom that my Aunt Lisa had painted before she married and gave up art school. What my mother is reacting to is something the book is telling her or some secret transmission she is receiving about the book. She raves and waves the book over her head as she goes around the house looking for matches, but since I have been encouraging her to give up smoking, I've flushed or dampened most of the books and tossed several boxes of Kents into my great-aunt's compost pile. Kick the habit! I screech, just like the insistent public service announcements on TV. It does no good, she keeps buying cigarettes. Now she can't find any matchbooks in the house. She fishes out a box from the crock by the fireplace, but they are damp. Even so, she tries to strike one several times but the sulfur tip just smears off like chalk. I wait for her to put my book down, but she won't let it go. She pulls out a chair and sits at the kitchen table, one hand holding the book to the tabletop, thinking. I go to the kitchen sink and run water to do the dishes. I will not get upset. I will ignore her. If she wants to see me cry, she'll have to do more than this.

"This is obscene. You won't do this to me. You won't get my daughter."

"You know it's a library book. Why don't I just return it?"

"Why don't I just kill this sick piece of trash!" she shrieks.

I watch her out of the corner of my eye from the kitchen sink as she moves about the house, looking for the best weapon to murder my book. Finally she takes the book and plunges it in the dishwater. She holds it down as if she is trying to drown it. I am screaming, furious, but I realize that it's all inside me, I'm standing still and silent, my hands clenched by my side. Once she is convinced the book is sufficiently dead, she lets it go. It floats like a fish to the surface. I take it out of the water and examine it. Its pages have turned glassy and thin; when I try to turn a page, the corner peels away and it tears without a sound. I set it on the edge of the sink, finish the dishes, smuggle the book outside, and put it in the shed under the rowboat to dry. A few days later it has warped to about three times its original size and looks like nothing I want to read. I steal a stone from my uncle's seawall and set it on top in the hope that the pages can be mashed flat. After several more days it becomes clear the book is ruined, and I am too shy and ashamed to return it that way to the library. I tell the librarian I have lost it, and she gives me a fine to take home, which, though not large, is more than the cost of the book. When I offer to try to just get another copy of the book, she refuses, saying that this is how it is done. So I do not pay, the library sends home notes, which I forge or throw away until finally my library borrowing privileges are revoked.

In order to feed my reading habit, I begin to steal library books. The books are usually small pocket paperbacks that can be easily hidden in my book bag or slipped down the front of my jeans. It is almost too easy to steal from the library. I never take my stolen books in the house but read them in my nest in the woods and then hide them in bread bags in the upside-down rowboat in our shed.

Once the books are in the bread bags in the heat and humidity of the shed, they mold and cannot be returned. So once my bread bag is full of books that are covered with the ashy spots of mildew and the pages blurred soft, I smuggle them to Aunt Pearline's compost heap. I take along a pine branch and gently probe the side; the lurid green bottleflies fling up and away but the yellow jackets and bees stay put, drunk from feeding on the juice of old tomatoes and watermelon rinds. Then I take the books, two or three at a time if they are small, and bury them in the dark heat that is the center of the pile.

Every few weeks Aunt Pearline drops off vegetables and flowers from her garden, tomatoes, Indian corn with stained-glass kernels, zinnias. Now they're all fertilized with her book-spiked compost. At first I am terrified that I will be caught, and when I'm not, I savor my secret: I am devouring books.

1975

*T*hat fall the rains begin. The cottage has no gutters and soon a dripline encircles our house like a moat. The earth fills with water until each step we take on the forest floor sinks our shoes into a sludge under the pine needles. Once the ground is saturated, the water pushes through the pine needles and holly leaves and floats them above the mud. Raindrops make the pine needles and ground look strangely alive, as if something is pushing up from underneath. We put pots around the house to catch the drips, and they ping out a gentle lulling tune.

Each tide is higher than the last, until the pier planks in our cove seem to float just above the waterline at the lowest tide and are submerged at the highest. I walk out of the cottage at high tide and I am amazed to see the cove has spilled out of its banks and halfway toward the cottage. The water is thin and gray. Minnows flick about the base of the holly tree and azalea bushes. Bits of trash have washed in too and snarl in the brush pile. Darby waves from her bedroom window and then puts her finger to her lips. A few minutes later she sneaks out the back door of her house and we walk to Griffins Beach. There's a big net with a dead dolphin tangled in it stinking on the shore.

"Is this a hurricane?" I ask.

"There was a hurricane. Or a tropical storm. If there's a hurricane, you leave. But we may flood. If it does flood maybe you guys can spend the night. I heard Mom talking about it. She told Dad that you guys can't stay in the cottage during a flood. And then Dad said that if the cottage did flood, then she could invite you guys up. So keep your fingers crossed."

"When's the next high tide?"

"It's later, nine or so tonight. Sheila wants to play dress up with Emma, but I thought we could play séance, if you don't think you'll be too scared. Wooooooooooo-oooh-boo!"

*   *   *

When I return to the cottage Mom is putting things up on blocks in anticipation of the flood. We turn the kitchen chairs upside down on the table like we do every Friday afternoon at school. Mom gets some bricks from the woodshed and we hoist up the sofa several inches off the floor. We take all the drawers out of our dressers and stack them on top like pickup sticks. We gathered all the toys we can find.

"How much water do you think we'll get?" I imagine the house flooding inside higher and higher so that I have to sit in the rafters. I imagine swimming inside the cottage like a giant swimming pool and having to hold my breath and dive down to get through the front door. I picture our flood like *The Poseidon Adventure.*

"I don't know."

"Have you ever been in a flood?"

"There were some little ones here, see the old watermark?" Mom shows me a dark wavery strip along the pine wall in the kitchen. "That's how high the water was." It comes up to my knee. I'm disappointed. I'd pictured the water coming in and floating into our clothes—my father's pants and hunting jacket in the closet, my mother's funky satin zebra nightgown—swelling with water and moving about the cottage in some sort of slow-motion *Fantasia* sequence.

"We should flip off the electricity and use candles, don't you think?"

"The water won't get high enough. We'll unplug the fridge and hot plate, but the water won't get to the outlets." The electrical system in the cottage is simple. Thick flat cords run along the very tops of the walls to the electrical outlets located there. Still I am worried we will get shocked.

"It'll be fun to use the candles, please. We can take a few from the war children's supply, can't we?"

Mom looks at me and grins. "Oh, why not?" Mom goes into the supply box and out comes a box of candles and Rose matches. I climb on the back of the sofa and flip the handle to the main power switch on the fuse box. Soon the cottage is aglow inside. This place is meant for just this sort of warmth and quiet. The soft light seems to calm all of us. We eat our hot dogs together at the kitchen table in silence while the world around us gets small and snug as we wait for disaster to strike.

I imagine the flood happening like a tidal wave or a flash flood—a sudden uprising of ocean pouring into our house. But the water rises in painfully slow increments.

"I'm gonna go check the water," I say to Mom at least every twenty minutes. I get the flashlight and head out in the dark toward the cove. This time I hit water before I get to the camellia tree, about fifty feet from the cottage. The shed is filling too, I can hear things bumping against the walls like boats at the dock. I walk farther out and listen. It is windy and the rain is still coming down, but you can't hear a bird or cricket or cicada. It's as if they have all drowned. There's the sizzle of rain and the eerie creak of branches overhead, but beneath those noises is a deep silence. It is not a wide-open silence, but something full and soft and ancient. In a way, I feel this gentle softness is the clouds come down to earth.

"Hey!" Darby is splashing through the woods in giant black boots and a rain poncho. "Mom and Dad say you guys can come over. Sheila is getting everything ready for the séance. C'mon, race you."

We slosh back through the woods to the cottage.

"Hey, Aunt Molly. Mom and Dad want you guys to come up and stay with us during the flood. Pack your toothbrushes and come on."

"Now, Darby. We'll be fine. Tell your mother that I don't need her charity. We're perfectly capable of taking care of ourselves."

"Please, Mom! ! ! It'll be fun." I want to play séance with

Sheila and Darby but I also want to take a bath. The cottage has only the metal ship shower but their house has two bathtubs, and I long to fill a bathtub high with bubbles and just stretch out. "You could take a bath . . ."

"Oh, sure," Darby says. "You can have my bed, Emma can take Sheila's, and we'll all sleep upstairs in the TV room. Please, Aunt Molly."

"Not yet. There's no water in the cottage, we're fine. I'll think about it. You go on home."

Darby shrugs and then calls over her shoulder to Mom, "-You'll see, Aunt Molly."

I walk Darby outside. "Don't worry, Gingie, we'll have our séance. Aunt Molly's just mad at Mom. I'll come back in a bit."

"Mom won't come. You know how she is."

"Look, Gingie, she'll have to come. She won't have a choice once the cottage floods. It's dangerous."

In times of real crisis Mom loves to rally to the occasion. Now that it is going to flood, Emma gets a bedtime story and is changed into a sweet terry-cloth gown with a cartoon duck sewn on each pocket. I put on one of Dad's old lawn-mowing T-shirts, which still smells of field grass and Speed Stick deodorant. Mom sits on the edge of my bed and brushes my hair the way she did when I was very young. "You should do one hundred strokes each night," she says. "And always rinse with vinegar so it will shine. We have good hair. Yours is so thick and soft, even though it's short. You're a little pixie." She strokes my hair with her fingertips and my whole body tingles. Each pore in my body breathes. I want to make this moment last forever. Just this: my head on my pillow, Mom peaceful and loving, her hand on my hair. This is the best feeling in the world.

*   *   *

I wake a little while later to go to the bathroom. I swing my feet over the edge of the bed and they land in water. I jerk them back into the bed and look at the floor. It's here! The cottage is flooding, there's about three inches on every floor. The cats are hunched and yowling in the rafters and Ralph is on the sofa. Emma is asleep in her bed.

Mom has the stereo on and is playing Grieg. The front door is flung open as if she is inviting the flood inside.

"Can we go to Darby's?"

"We're fine," Mom says, and keeps striding around the house humming along with the stereo.

"I think it's dangerous. How high will the water get?"

"We're protected, Gingie."

I notice the overhead lights are on.

"You should turn off the electricity. There's water in the house. We can get electrocuted." I jump on the sofa.

"Leave it on. We're fine, I told you."

"No way!"

Right then Aunt Lisa appears. Thank God.

She taps her flashlight against the door frame to get Mom's attention. Mom is dancing in the water, her face titled toward the reflection of the water on the rafters.

Aunt Lisa looks at me and then bangs the flashlight harder. "Mom!" I scream.

"What, what?" Then she sees Aunt Lisa.

"Molly, please come up to the house. We've fixed cookies for the girls and have a bed all made for you. You don't have to stay here through this."

Mom doesn't move toward the door. "We're doing just fine. We don't need your charity."

Aunt Lisa clenches her jaw. "Molly, it's not charity. You're family, and this is not a good place for you to be during a flood. Stay with us tonight and I'll help you guys clean up tomorrow." She pauses and stares at the floodwater on our floors. "Please, Molly."

"Go home."

"Molly, please. At least let me take the girls up to the house. This is not right."

"You need to leave my property now. Do you understand?"

"Mom! Can't we go? It'll be a slumber party."

"No."

"Molly, look——"

"You look. Get out of my goddamn house."

Aunt Lisa turns purple and pulls her lips in tight to her face. She looks like she is going to let Mom have it, and I can't wait, but she chickens out. "Have it your way," she says and heads back to her house. "You'll see," she says, just like Darby.

"I want to go! Why can't we go?"

"Because I said so."

"I hate you. You're selfish."

Mom pauses and sits on the sofa next to me. "No, hon. We have to stay here. What if the war children come tonight? Who'll take care of them?"

We sit on the sofa and I see a minnow dart underneath the sofa. We stick our feet in the water and it comes out to nibble our toes. Soon two others appear. I slosh through the house and find one small live crab and two dead ones, floating belly up. A pencil watts by and scraps of paper and a high bounce ball I'd lost the summer before bob around the room. The reflection of the lights in the house off the water make everything seem alive. The warpy light is on the rafters, the walls, the furniture, and our faces. It's like a funhouse in here. This was wilder than any séance with my cousins.

Mom grabs the Magic Eight Ball off the shelf behind us. "Oh, Magic Eight Ball, will the war children come tonight?"

Better not tell you now, comes the reply in the inky window.

"You ask something."

"Oh Magic Eight Ball," I say, "will the cottage be swept away in the flood?"

Outlook not so good.

"I didn't ask it the right way. Oh, Magic Eight Ball, will the flood go away soon?"

Signs point to yes.

Right then Emma wakes and screams to see her green scoop and toy tiger floating in the middle of the room.

"Can I get in the water too?"

I look at Mom.

"Sure!"

Emma tucks her blankie under her pillow and wades in. "-It's so warm," she smiles. The water is almost waist-deep on her and her nightgown fans out around her like a flower.

"Hi there, baby duck!" Mom says and holds out her arms.

"Ring around the rosie," Emma sings and watches her dress as she twirls in the water. Mom takes our hands. We dance in circles in the water, around and around. I imagine we are in a whirlpool and will be sucked away to somewhere strange and exotic. Oz. Or maybe the Bermuda Triangle. We dance until we are dizzy and then Emma sits on the sofa. "Waltz!" Mom yelps and changes the record on the stereo to "The Blue Danube." Mom takes my hands and we begin, awkward and slow, but then glide through four cycles. Emma claps her hands.

"You lead," she says and we alternate back and forth.

When I wake early the next morning, the tide has retreated and most of the flood has left the house. I go outside to inspect our property. The ground is still puddled with water and covered with seaweed and mud. There are sea snails trailing on the holly tree and dead crabs and live ones are trapped together in small pools. Silver minnows lay scattered across the land like lost coins. Nothing is in its rightful place.

"Well," Mom sighs as she comes outside to see the damage. "We made it through the night."

My eyes sting with tears, and my emotion takes me by surprise. I want to run away. I want to fling my arms around my mother's neck and have her carry me to bed. Maybe I want to feel safe again and know I never will. But I don't move. I just stand there until the storm inside me passes so I can speak.

"Let's eat," I say and lead us back to the cottage. "We've got a big day ahead of us."

2000

*M*y father drove in from Virginia Beach as soon as he discovered what had happened. We hauled out the furniture and scraped the mud from the floors. The flood was hardly newsworthy unless you happened to be living in substandard housing near the water. It wasn't the sort of rollicking, wavy affair that got lots of play on the news channels and caused folks in Sandbridge to fear that their beach houses would be swept away.

My father recalls that at this time he was wild with anger and fear. He was slowly beginning to see that my mother was truly never going to return to Virginia Beach. At that time, he felt his options went like this: He could leave his wife, and us with her, and seek a divorce. He could move us back to Virginia Beach, and then she could seek custody and would doubtless get it. Women did in those days. Or he could move in with us, get a job in the area, and look after his family the way he had promised in his wedding vows. Could things get worse? He would have done just as well to ask the Magic Eight Ball.

Dad announced that he intended to find a job in the area and move in with us as soon as possible. Mom flung her arms around his neck as if she were welcoming home a soldier. That day he insisted that the windows get scraped clean. My mother objected, but Dad said we had to get blinds or curtains. I left the cottage and when I came back I watched Dad strip the last few windows clean. It was unceremonious. He wiped each pane with a thick coat of orange paint stripper and then used a flat-edged scraper. The paint sloughed off like shed skin. He left the paint on the window in the bathroom, since it was a private place anyway, and that was that. You could still see little edges of black paint on the panes like the border on funeral stationery. I suppose our outline on the windows gave folks the same sort of inkling that there was bad news inside.

1976

*I*t takes Dad over six months to find a job near Kechotan because so many people are out of work. So he spends part of the week in Virginia Beach and part with us at the cottage. On Saturday mornings my father comes down, the station wagon loaded with groceries he has picked up, mainly things we can cook on the hot plate. Cold cuts, sandwich meats, hot dogs, and cans of soup. He brings lots of Coke. Mom and I unpack the groceries, riffling through the bags to see what treats are inside. Dad scoops Emma in his arms, tosses her up in the air, and nuzzles her until she laughs her big belly laugh and squeals for more. I notice this time that Dad sighs deeply when he looks around the cottage. I realize all at once that he thinks he is doing something wrong. There's a slump in his shoulders that I've never noticed before and an unwillingness to look me in the eye for too long.

The weekends are filled with chores and after the groceries are unloaded, Dad and I pick up the trash that Mom and I had set outside in big green plastic bags and load those into the back of the station wagon. Then we head for the dump. Just the two of us.

As we drive into Messick, the first thing I always notice is how the houses get older and more spindly-looking; the exterior of some places makes the rooms look as if they once fell apart from each other and then were quickly reattached so that now the boards don't line up properly. Some of the porches are held up not with pillars or columns, but with the same sorts of long cedar poles that you see on old-timers' piers. Most have outhouses. Many have no power lines strung up to them from the street and seem oddly adrift. All the time, people are out on their front porches, watermen and their families mostly: mending nets, snapping beans. Often there is a dog chained in the yard, a car up on blocks. It's just the same as the picture in our history book that talks about poverty and the Great Depression. When I go through Messick, it doesn't look as if much has changed.

The landfill is the only place around us that has hills. These are gassy and smelly and made of years upon years of trash. The hills gleam with slick green Glad bags, but atop them lie crab shells boiled red and husked from the local cannery, broken lawn chairs with torn madras straps, split plastic bags of soiled Pampers. The air here is moist, one long wavy stench of heat and meat. The dumpsite isn't far from the crab house and the fishing docks. It sits right on the water and if I hold my nose and look past the festering mounds of garbage I can see sea grass rippling in the marsh like a distant prairie. But when I remove my hand and stare in front of me the plain infectedness of the dump just about knocks me out. The soil here is foul and sends thick rainbow slicks into the water that are actually kind of pretty until they go dark and crusty and make the mouth of the marsh foam a constant nasty brown.

*   *   *

The dump man drives a tractor and waves us to the spot where we are to unload. We get out and toss our trash in with the rest. Seagulls laugh and bob and swirl in the air around us, those ugly yellow-billed dirt-speckled ones, and gulls on the hills pick through the rotting trash, shaking pieces in their beaks like bull terriers. Dad points to a seagull with one foot and one eye that looks like a pirate bird. "Hey," Dad says. "What the hell happened to ol' Jonathan Livingston Seagull there?" I roll my eyes. "Jon, you're not looking too good there, buddy." I haven't read the book, even though everybody has a copy in their house.

We stand and watch as a hawk flies off to line its nest with the plastic rings that yoke six packs. The seagulls screech and dive toward a bucket of Kentucky Fried Chicken bones, picking through the paper and foil. We watch as four speckled gulls yank and gouge at one another over a ragged chicken breast. I can't imagine what the weeping Indian on the litter commercial would do if he ever saw this place.

My father puts his arm around my neck and gives me a squeeze. "Your granddaddy used to say he'd seen just about everything traveling around with the Merchant Marine and after all his time around the world, he knew one thing for sure—war won't be our ruin, we'll simply pollute ourselves right off the face of the earth." It's easy enough to believe.

As we drive out we pass by a separate dump for cars on the

same grounds. Here's where you can go and rip out a car seat, or get a part if you need one, and there is always someone here doing that. Every other week or so we see the same young fellow, wearing a short-sleeved work shirt with Ezra stitched over the pocket, taking pieces from Chevrolets. My father would look at me and sing a few lines from Johnny Cash's "One Piece at a Time," about a fellow who built his own Cadillac from stolen parts. I always shushed him, but today he cups his hands and sings out to Ezra. "Hey, man, 'I got it one piece at a time,' and Ezra squints back at my father and then smiles and sings back to us: 'And it didn't cost me a dime.'"

I am always impressed at how good my father is with people. He has this ability to adapt and talk with everyone from watermen to businessmen. Even people he doesn't like, like Uncle Chuck, he still finds them interesting. Folks sense that about him. People always treat Dad with respect.

We drive back from the dump with the windows rolled down to get the smell out of the car and our noses. Dad asks about school and I lie and say that I am doing fine and enjoying my classes. I ask when we're moving back to Virginia Beach. I ask him the same question every visit and the answer is always the same, "I don't know." But when I ask this time he says that he has found a job in Newport News and will start in a few weeks. The town house in Virginia Beach is for sale. He tells me Mom isn't going to move back and that all this traveling between two houses is just no good for anyone. This will be good, because we'll all be able to live together as a family in one house.

I feel my insides wobble. I know that we are living in Ke-

chotan, and that I am in school here, and that I have never
even so much as written a letter to Cammie Rickleman in Virginia Beach, but Virginia Beach is Home. Though I sort of
want to see how things are going to turn out in the secret war,
or even see if the secret war will happen, I don't want Kechotan to be home. And so I began to cry.

"Hey, hey, calm down, it'll be O.K." My father pulls the
station wagon over to the side and I hurl my head against
his chest and just sob. When I was little and I would get upset
I couldn't stop my body from crying even after I stopped
wanting to cry. My father would always come upstairs and
give me a glass of water and make me take sips until I could
breathe again. Sometimes I couldn't stop sobbing and my
teeth would chatter against the rim of the glass so violently I
thought it would break in my mouth. Now I cry until I can't
see and I can't breathe. My snot covers the breast pocket of his
plaid shirt. He just hugs me and pats my back. "Let it all out,
sweetie. Just get it all out."

When I am done, he takes my face in his big red hands and
wipes underneath my eyes with his thumbs. He pulls out his
handkerchief from his front pocket, folds it to a clean patch
and wipes the snot off my nose and tells me to blow. Then he
tucks the hankie in his pocket.

"You didn't look at it," I tell him.

"What?"

"You didn't look in your handkerchief!" My father makes a
bad habit of blowing his nose and then inspecting the results
like he's reading tea leaves.

"You!" He sticks his hand in the crook of my neck, my

most ticklish spot, and I squeal and wiggle until he pulls his hand free from the clamp of my cheek and shoulder.

He starts the car and we head back toward the cottage. I start thinking how wonderful it will be to have my father living with us all the time.

"I've got a few things I need to take care of in Virginia Beach this weekend, what with putting the town house up for sale. How about you come up with me. Visit with Cammie?"

He's read my mind.

*   *   *

After almost a year away, returning to our home in Virginia Beach is strange. How is it possible we've been gone so long? The rows of town houses are all the same but the concrete and asphalt landscape, which I had never paid attention to before, now seems compact and hard. My memory of my life here was colliding with life here without me. Somehow, I expected Virginia Beach would remain the same, just as I left it, like a little snow globe village come to life whenever I picked it up.

I call over to Tammie's house to play. But Tammie herself has changed. She is tall and her red hair has grown long and has darkened. She speaks of children and teachers I don't know. We try to do the things we used to do together, like looking through her sister's diary, but her sister had stopped writing in it months before. The last entry says, Dear Diary: I hope that Tammie stops *Reading you!!!* Her sister has taken down the poster of Tania and now has a picture of some rock star on her wall, with long blonde curls and an oily chest.

We don't know what to say to each other, so we go to the 7-Eleven and buy bomb pops to put in our mouths. We sit together on the curb and count cigarette butts. Then Tammie says she forgot that she has a dance lesson and has to go. I am confused to feel both relief and embarrassment at my relief. All of sudden I want nothing more than to flee this place and go home, to the cottage.

I walk to the town house to pack up a few things. In my desk drawer I remember that I left a pet frog I smuggled into the house. He is still there, hard and odorless, and dry. He doesn't look exactly the way I left him, but he is pretty close. I feel a knife stab of guilt and then think he looks kind of cool, so I take him to Dad.

"Aw, gee, Virginia," my father says when he sees him. "Poor little guy."

I find a little box, put in some cotton balls, and tuck him inside. "When are we going home?" I ask my father.

"Isn't there anyone else you want to see? You didn't play with Cammie long."

"She has a dance lesson. Alita's moved. The Farabaughs are out of town." Everybody is somewhere else. And this place where I once lived and played now seems dried up and dull in comparison to our life in Kechotan. "How much longer do we have to stay?"

"Help me get these tools in the trunk and then we can head on."

Back at the cottage, I feel calmer. This is my home and I know it is my home now. I take out the little white pasteboard box from my shirt pocket and give it to my mother.

"Look what Gingie left behind," Dad says as she opens the box and screams and laughs.

"I just forgot about him. I think he starved to death."

"Oh, but he's perfectly preserved." She taps on his skin and his body makes a sad hollow sound. "I've never seen anything like it." My mother is delighted by my frog. And there is something funny about him, once I get past the fact that I have killed him; he is kind of cute, so perfectly preserved in his scrawny state. She gives him a place of honor on our mantelpiece, along with two old lanterns and a broken kit clock whose hands hang permanently defeated at six-thirty. He becomes an odd sort of family totem. Our very own mummy. We name him Tut.

2000

I want to lie. To say that our lives in Kechotan were awful and horrible all the time. But the truth is that there were days it wasn't so bad, and even times it was flat-out fun. Yet, if I tell the moments when my mother and father and I laughed and picked crabs over newspaper at the table, or the time my mother rescued our dog Ralept off the highway, that's not really the truth, or it's only part of it. Those years were some also one of the blackest and most awful I can imagine a family enduring.

Still, we had our moments.

1974

We are stuck in traffic because of the gas lines. People turn off their cars and open their doors. The four-lane boulevard looks like a migration of steel-winged Chevrolets. About a mile ahead, wavering in the dull nickel-colored heat glaze, is the Esso station causing all the trouble.

My mother reaches into her purse and hands Emma her green plastic flour scoop. Mom is thrilled with Emma. She is quiet and sweet.

"I'm hungry," I complain and slam the backseat with my sandals. My father hands me a stick of Juicy Fruit. He's just given up smoking. I tell him ten, twenty, thirty times a day: Kick the habit, kick the habit. Now I am determined to clean up my parents' cussing by inventing a rule that requires a one-cent contribution for each bad word uttered. Each time someone curses I remind them to put a Penny in the Pot.

"The gum's melty."

"It's fine, Gingie."

"It's disgusting."

"Give it back."

"Gum is not food. I said I was hungry."

"You're going to have to wait like the rest of us."

"But I am hungry."

"So swallow the goddamn gum."

"Penny in the Pot."

"Fine." He flips a penny over his shoulder and into the backseat.

I pop the gum in my mouth and my father holds out his hand for the wrapper.

"I'm bored."

Silence.

I look at Emma, big brown eyes open, quiet, but taking in everything. She is a good baby. Good babies are pretty and don't need much attention and so they get the most.

I climb over the seat and stick my feet out the back window of our Car.

"Can I get out?"

"No."

"I won't go anywhere. I just want to get out of the car. I'm hot."

"We're all hot."

"I'm boiling"

"Nathan, it's hot," my mother chimes in.

"It's just as hot outside. Hot as hell. Hell, it's hotter."

"That's two pennies!"

I open the door and stand barefoot on the blazing asphalt, which at first feels warm, then marvelously hot, and then

into-the-bones unbearable. I jump from foot to foot and re-
trieve my flip-flops.

"See?" my father says and shakes his head.

None of the cars is moving. Folks are walking up and down
the little paths between cars. Some people have decided to
tailgate and are making the best of it. Others pace and curse.
A group of surfers take off their shirts and oil up to catch
some sun.

When I go on car trips with my parents I usually lie in the
backseat; the telephone poles and trees and other cars growling past make the light in the car seem all flickery, like a home
movie. Now the cars are silent, except for the Fords ticking in
the heat like time bombs, the slap of flip-flops, the dragging
Dutch-shoe clomp of Dr. Scholl's.

"What a beautiful beast!" My mother crosses her arms and
leans out the window. "That's a magnificent animal, Nathan.
Just look."

In the median strip just ahead is an enormous gray dog,
with a heavy head and trunk, caved-in belly, and legs as long
as Tina Turner's.

"He's the size of a small pony."

Our last dog had been a handsome Scottie named Torkle
McCorkle. This is a dog I can ride!

"Oh, look at him, no one has been caring for him. See that
man is trying to get him into his car. That dog is a stray." The
man calls and pats his thigh. He snaps his fingers and makes
kissy noises. The dog ignores him.

"Why that animal is hurt!" my mother cries.

The man reaches out one hand and sets it on the dog's

head. The animal's black gums curl back and he bares his teeth. The man's fingers pull in as he steps back deliberately—he knows everyone is watching him. He puts his hands in his pockets and says something to his wife. Car doors begin to slam ahead of us and some cars move several feet forward. The man shrugs and gets in the car.

"Nathan." The desire in her voice is unmistakable. Her eyes on the dog. "Let's pull over and see if we can get Ralph in the car."

"Good God, Molly, you've named the mutt Ralph. Stop it. He's been dumped. Probably eats five pounds of food a day. He's not hurt. He doesn't seem to want to go anywhere."

Ralph sits in the median strip and begins licking his balls. His pink belly is crawling with fleas.

"Oh, Nathan," my mother pleads. "Let's try."

"For chrissakes, that filthy thing isn't coming home with us."

"Penny in the Pot."

Suddenly my father gets out of the car and goes over to talk to Ralph. He doesn't budge, but when my father reaches out to pat him, Ralph sniffs his hand. Dad walks back to the car. "That dog stinks. He's nasty. And he doesn't want to move."

"See if you can get him in the car, Nathan."

"I am not going to carry that thing."

"Oh, Nathan."

"Oh, Christ."

"Penny—"

My father reaches in, grabs my hand, and jams in a dollar bill. "It's an advance. Now zip it."

He stalks around to the back of the wagon and lifts the door. "Here's your chance, dog. Free ride."

My father makes a clicking noise with his tongue that sounds better suited to horses.

Ralph looks at my father then at the open door that leads to the back of our station wagon, and in one leap, hops in. My mother and I cheer, Emma claps her hands, and my father slams the door, dusts off his hands, and swaggers back. He starts the engine and traffic begins to lurch. Gas fumes ripple the air.

"Oh, Nathan." My mother leans over to kiss his cheek.

"Pee-UUU! ! ! ! He's smells terrible."

"He'll be fine after a bath," Dad says.

"Oh, Gawd! He's disgusting."

My mother turns on the dashboard fan.

"But he's smart. He waited for us. He knows a sucker when he sees one."

The almost-bitten man looks back jealously at our dog. My father has won: He got Ralph in the car no problemo. Dad and Ralph seem meant for each other. Ralph finishes chewing a red oozy spot on his back and begins breathing on my neck. His enormous pink tongue lolls out of his mouth and he drools on the vinyl seats.

"He's spitting on me!"

On the way home my father tells us all the usual things in TV-dad fashion. We'll have to try to find the owner of the dog. We'll take out an ad in the paper. Dogs like this, Dad says, usually aren't abandoned. As this last bit came out of his mouth it was clear he knew that no one in their right mind would lay claim to this animal.

My mother unlocks the front door and Ralph walks right in like he owns the place. He sniffs around the furniture. Then very slowly he cocks one leg and begins peeing on my parents' new sofa.

He's home.

2000

*D*ad got a job with Blue Heron Properties selling commercial real estate in Newport News and began living with us fulltime. He hated the job, but it was a job. My freedom outside the cottage increased. I went for long walks and had secret hiding places in the woods, beaches, and sheds. My favorite place was deep in the trash pines a quarter mile up the road, where the grave of my great-grandfather and two small, children's graves were located in an overgrown tangle of periwinkle and pine straw. The children's headstones were pocked white marble, the names and dates worn smooth. Even on cold days, I would go out there and hunker down in my snug little nest and dream while the sky and leaves moved above me.

Mom's reaction to Dad's daily presence in the house was at first a straightening up. It started with her hair. In the mornings used both hands to twist it—as if wringing out a wet shirt—into a rope. And then she twirled it around and around until it looked like a honeybun. Then she'd get a mouthful of bobby pins and practically staple the thing to the back of her head. She looked older like this and not quite like my mother. She started wearing work clothes, slacks and plain shirts. Her satin zebra gown went to the closet, as did her little sundresses and winter coats. She tried not to discuss the secret war, especially in Dad's presence, but her efforts in this direction led to frustration and then to secrecy. She kept her notebook hidden in the breadbox and confined her war efforts to the hours when my father was at work. This clandestine routine produced at first a hightened urgency, but after a while even this settled down some and since this was as good as things had been for a while, we all set about trying our hardest to act like the life we were now leading was normal. Mom kept house and made suppers and took care of Emma. Dad mowed the field and cleared the thickets and tried to winterize the house as best he could. I guess during this time Mom went into a sort of remission.

Yet I couldn't let go of the secret war just like that. I tried to keep it alive and set about trying to speed things up.

1976

I am finished memorizing the first aid manual and I tell Mom that I want to help her hunt for clues, so I should be reading mystery books, something I do anyway. She agrees that this would be a very good thing to do. The added bonus is that she will leave me alone for weeks and I can bring any book I want in the house, as long as it has a Nancy Drew or Hardy Boys cover on it. All for the war effort. I don't identify with any of the characters in the books. But I do envy them always having something to hunt. In these books there is always a mystery and one that can be solved, eventually, through hard work and breaking the rules in a minor way that no one really gets punished for, because, after all, the mystery is solved and the caper wrapped up.

As I read all of these stories I see again everywhere there are mysteries and clues that will lead me to the secret children. A bit of string, a sheet of quilted silver paper from a stick of gum, these things will set me on the path to my new friends.

But no matter how much I look the war children refuse to reveal themselves. Sometimes though, I lean against a tree and feel a child on the other side, listening hard, desperate not to be detected. Breathless, unmoving, unblinking.

Perhaps, I tell my mother one afternoon, the secret children are hiding from us; they have become scared traveling all by themselves and are now wild and living in our woods, or in the marsh. There are stranger stories, of children raised by wolves or on their own, living on the fringes. We've all heard of children in Korea and Vietnam who ran into the hills and came out only when they felt it was safe, to get a scrap of food or steal a blanket. Mom says she thinks I might be right and says also that children tend to only trust other children, so I should try to make friends with the war children before I bring any back to the field hospital. I ponder where these children might be hiding and how I can lure them to me.

I set up a small camp for myself near my great-grandfather's grave. I take my pocketknife and carve my initials in a tree and below it I leave a pack of nabs and a Coke. I set out one of Emma's toys, a plush spotted puppy with a black vinyl nose. I hunker down in a vine-covered canopy underneath the trash pines and hide and read. Wait. Sleep and dream.

The war children are not so easy to outsmart. They never take my food, so I begin eating it. When I run out of Nancy Drews to read, I move on to other books. Greek and Roman mythology, Little Women, the Little House series. I carry them out under an enamors canopied azalea bush during the day and if I haven't finished by the evening, I take them with me to bed.

It's not yet July fourth, the Bicentennial, when she arrives. I don't remember how she appears, whether I am in a dream or awake, or in some place in between, but there she is, the silent girl on the other side of tree. She looks like a ghost girl, thin and pale and barefoot. Her hair is lank and long enough for her to hide behind when she likes. She's dirty and tired and her hands are cut.

"Who are you?" I ask her, but she just looks at me.

"Are you hurt?" She doesn't move forward, but stands and stares at me for a long time. Then she sits on my great-grandfather's headstone.

"Are you thirsty?" I set my Coke in front of her and then back away. My heart is pounding in my chest. I want to grab her and catch her, but I know I have to stay calm. She reminds me of the wild kittens who live in the abandoned garage up the street. My dad lured one out, but it took weeks.

The ghost girl looks so sad. And also not real. It's in the slowness of the way she moves, and how she won't speak, how her feet in the brush never make a sound. I have read about shock in the first aid and survival books, and I wonder if she has come from some battle in the secret war.

She gets up, looking at me the whole time, and picks up the bottle of Coke. She watches me as she drinks.

"Are there other children? Are you hungry?" I give her the two packs of crushed nabs I have in my bag and set them before her. She takes them.

"We've been waiting for you. My mother and I have clothes and supplies. I'll bring you some shoes and some Bactine. Wait here, O.K.?"

I run home and get shoes, Bactine, Band-Aids, and a pair of jeans and a T-shirt. I stuff them all in my bag.

"How's it going?" Mom asks me.

I'm terrified. Does she know? I don't want to bring the ghost girl home. I found her. She's mine. I tell myself that no one can tell when I am lying. They can only guess.

"It's fine. I just want to get stuff together. In case."

"That's good planning," she says. She doesn't know. She can't see inside me.

I run all the way back to my great-grandfather's grave but the girl is gone. I look around and see no sign of her. But she was here. I saw her. She will come back, I think, but as I think this, I know she'll never let me see her again.

I go to the pine tree and sit and close my eyes. Breathe. Breathe. Then I feel her, on the other side of the tree. She's back, quiet, listening from the other side. Just like me.

2000

*P*erhaps the most unsettling thing regarding my mother's "remission" was its suddenness. With Dad around and in front of other adults, she was able to act the part of the responsible parent and spouse. She made suppers, fixed up the cottage, signed forms that came home from school. But when there were no adults around she was unreliable. Sometimes my mother would seem normal. Other times the switch would just go off in her head and she would come after me or my sister with some relentless tirade of accusations that we simply learned to endure until she wore herself out. When we lived at the cottage, my sister recalls that she grew to distrust what my mother said, because her words never matched her actions. Like me, she became a watcher and a listener, trying to see in advance what my mother's next move might be, in case she needed to escape. She recalls being forced to eat a bowl of cereal crawling with ants. Another time, my mother gave my sister a glass of Clorox to drink instead of a glass of milk. My sister drank some and then couldn't breathe. I picked up the glass and smelled bleach. I screamed at my mother, and it seemed to take her a while before she realized what had happened and then she cracked a raw egg and poured it down Emma's throat. My mother was screaming and crying. A few minutes later Emma vomited. When the story was recounted later to my father and aunt and uncle it was that Emma had gotten into the Clorox and that my mother had kept her head and thought fast. It's difficult for me to remember my mother taking me on night maneuvers and giving Emma a glass of bleach and not speculate whether she wanted to hurt us or kill us.

I guess the question I ask myself the most is why didn't I tell on Mom. Why, when she treated me and my sister with contempt, violence, or just neglected us, didn't I scream and shout and make a fuss until someone did something? I knew something was really wrong and knew that my sister and I saw the worst of it and yet I was too scared. Maybe I didn't want to make things worse than they already were. Maybe like the adults around us, we saw things that didn't make sense and we felt helpless, so we ignored them. Maybe there's no answer or reason here that will ever make sense.

1976

*7*he old-timers say beachcombing's best right after the Indian Pipe pushes up," Chuck says and pours a can of STP into the little outboard. The water right around us foams brown and then slicks out in a thin, torn rainbow. "But Aunt Lisa saw two waterspouts moving downriver after the storm last night. They wore themselves out on Cow Island. Can't ask for better beachcombing conditions."

Chuck tosses the can toward the pier but it misses. Dad reaches over and tries to fish it out with a paddle. "It'll wash up," Chuck grunts. Dad slides the paddle back in place.

Dad leans over me and tightens the straps of my mildewed lifejacket so I have to sit up straight or it digs into my ribs.

"Is that too much?" he asks. His face is next to mine and I can see a small red scab beside the mole on his chin. I'd forgotten how he always cuts himself shaving. When he leaves in the mornings I go into the bathroom and stir up his whiskers and the aftershave smell in the drain. "Too much?"

I shake my head. "Just right."

He pulls Darby's and Sheila's too. He puts on his new plastic-smelling jacket and Chuck pulls the motor. "Toss another down," he yells up to Aunt Lisa and Mom. Their mouths laugh.

"Chuck won't wear one," Aunt Lisa bends down and shouts through her cupped hands. "Never has." Her binoculars hit her hard in the chest when she straightens up.

"Well, you get me the spare, Molly." Dad waves Mom toward the fishing shed. Just as she sails the jacket to the boat, Chuck pulls off. The preserver rocks in our wake. Our mothers close their eyes and shake their heads as we curve out of the cove.

I pull the collar of my sweater over my chapped mouth. I'm not used to being on the water in the cold weather. Darby hands me her tube of Chap Stick and I draw a big circle around my lips and then fill it in with the pinkish wax. When I hand it back to her, she slices off the tip with her long thumbnail and flicks it over the edge of the boat. "Germs," she explains.

"I remember when I was in the Army," Dad says. "We did some maneuvers and they told us how to survive if you fell off a boat into cold water."

Chuck spits in our wake.

"The best thing to do is to curl up in a little ball. Knees to your chest. Well, this is the best thing to do if you're in cold water and there's no land, nothing to hold on to, and nobody likely to rescue you for a while. Put your knees to your chest, and keep your head tucked to your chest. That way all of your warmth stays with you in a little pocket."

"Makes it kind of hard to breathe with your head underwater. Don't you think, girls?" I look at Darby and Sheila. Chuck doesn't like us to talk too much on the boat.

"Ah, see. But here's the trick. You need to hold your nose while you're underwater. Because the cold water can get up your nose and you'll start bleeding to death. But every so often all you have to do is roll your face up out of the water to take a breath. It's not a big deal, you're right near the surface. This way you stay warm and don't expend a lot of energy. You can survive a long time, depending on the water temperature of course."

"But what if help comes and they see you in that dead-man's float?" Sheila asks. "What if help just goes away?"

Chuck turns his head and looks at the hawks nesting in a nearby buoy.

"Well, you've got to learn to control your thoughts. It's best to do things like your multiplication tables. But sometimes you could be out there so long you start to daydream. But try to control them. Dreaming that you see a bunch of VW Beetles on the waves is O.K. Dreaming you are a fish is not. Keep in mind that you and the ocean are separate—and it's stronger. Don't let go of yourself. As soon as you do"— Dad snaps his fingers,—"it'll take you."

I ask Chuck, "Do you know any survival tricks in case we fall off the boat?"

"Never fell off a boat," he says. "Then I never was in the Army."

"Well, it's good advice," Dad says and winks at me. I make sure I smile.

*   *   *

131

Chuck pulls the little boat onto the sand as far as he can and sinks the anchor. Dad helps us out of the boat. We each put our arms around Dad's neck and he carries us one by one out of the boat to the dry sand. I'm the last to be set on shore and he gives me a special kiss in the part of my hair.

"Miss Ruth remembers someone got his leg blown off here," I say.

"Lord," Chuck whines, "I don't know how that story keeps going. They cleaned up this place years ago. You're not going to find much of that now."

He takes out a plastic tackle box and hands out old pillowcases and toothbrushes. "Then again, it mighta happened," he says to me. "Maybe you should watch your step. Boom!" he yells right in my ear.

I close my eyes but I don't jump. "Very funny," I say and walk onto the island. No one lives here anymore but you can tell people come here all the time. Old burnt sticks washed over by sand. Styrofoam cups from the 7-eleven and old trash caught in the sea grass.

There's nothing out here that belongs in Chuck's tall display case. Everything Chuck collects looks like it is store-bought or stolen from The Mariners' Museum in Newport News. White clay pipes with long unbroken stems. Matching mortar and pestle for grinding corn. A set of four arrowheads, each one longer than the last, that look cut from the same rock. And on one shelf a collection of rhinoceros beetles, their blue still so deep it looks wet, their little pincers sharp. I know I won't find anything that perfect here.

Darby and Sheila walk toward me. Sheila's taken off her shoes and socks and she's wading in the surf.

"See how the waves and sand give you the best pedicure? Your toenails are just white and beautiful. You don't need polish or anything." She holds up one long foot for us to admire. "Bet those city girls don't know about this."

Sheila has just started modeling for the Leggett in Newport News. They set up a little stage in the mall and all the girls get their makeup and hair done beforehand at the Revlon counter. Darby and I went to see her last week and the woman doing makeup did me and Darby, too. She put lots of eyeliner on me and three different colors of eye shadow on Darby. Her eyes are shiny and cool like butterfly wings. When I looked in the mirror I expected to appear different, instead my face just looked dirty. I wiped it off.

"You can make a lot of money if you've got the right look," Sheila says.

"How much do you get?" I ask. "For one of those shows."

"Oh, that's for free. You have to do those to get discovered. All sorts of talent scouts come out and look for girls."

Darby sits on the sand beside me and starts digging with her hands.

"Is that how you do it?" I whisper and start digging my own hole.

"I've found two arrowheads and an old medicine bottle this way. I dig inland. I've always found the best stuff before I hit water."

"But I get paid twenty-five dollars for the next show. We get to be mannequins for Casual Corner."

Darby rolls her eyes.

"What do you mean you get to be a mannequin?"

Sheila walks back from us, holds her hands in front of her

like she's about to accept a present or a bouquet of flowers, tosses her head to the side, and freezes.

"I don't get it."

"That's all there is to get," Darby says and stabs a stick into the mound of sand beside her.

"Huh?"

"Look, stupid," Sheila says. "You have to be a live mannequin. You have to stand still as a statue. You try to fool people into thinking you're not real. You can't breathe much and you try not to blink except when nobody's looking. It's really hard."

"I saw you blink."

"Well it'll be easier there. It's windy here. And there's a trick, too, that they told us. You just look at the little reflection of yourself in the glass, you know, stop yourself from looking at the people looking at you."

"And they pay you for this? Don't they have mannequins?"

Darby starts laughing and Sheila sits down beside us and claws at the sand.

"Forget it, Gingie." Sheila says and hooks her hair behind her ears.

"I'm sorry," I tell her, though I'm not really. "I think you'll make a good model."

"Really?"

"You're really pretty. Like Mom, everybody says so."

Sheila stands up and shakes her pants legs. Sand blows in our faces. "I don't look a thing like Aunt Molly," she snaps and storms off.

"Oh, you just have to ignore her," Darby says. "She's a pain in the butt."

* * *

Dad waves from down the beach. Darby and I wave back. "He wants us to come down there," Darby says. "Race you." And she's off, arms pumping. Dad stands with his arms out to his sides. Our finish line. I run close to the shore, where the sand is firm, so fast my legs stop feeling anything and I am just gliding. I catch her and pass her and hit Dad's hand at least two seconds before her.

"Slowpoke."

She's bent over, hands on her knees, gasping. "You wait. Next year or so you'll have to stop being such a tomboy."

"Look at that," Dad says, pointing to a little gully in the sand that runs from the shore to the scrubby bushes farther inland. "That's where one of the waterspouts ran aground last night. Cool, huh? Chuck's already found a hatchet head and a little blue bottle. I don't know how he does it. You girls find anything?"

Darby shrugs.

Dad reaches in his pocket. "I found these." He has two bullets and a shark's tooth. "I could find more with that metal detector, but Chuck thinks that's cheating. We'll come out here by ourselves sometime."

"I'd like that," I say and give him a big grin. Dad frowns and then hugs me to him with one arm.

"You girls go get Sheila. Almost time to head back for lunch."

Sheila has the binoculars and we stand on the shore and point them across the water to her house. Even with the binoculars things look small. Mom and Aunt Lisa are in the yard hanging sheets on the line. Four clothespins a sheet is the way Aunt Lisa does it. And the sheets are never wrung out, always hung sopping wet on the line. That way, she says, they get softer and smoother than any iron could ever get them. I look through the binoculars and Darby waves, but they can't see us unless they're looking though the binoculars at the same time. To them, we're just specks.

Darby has dug a little hole near the shore and is scrubbing her find with a toothbrush.

"Anything good?"

"I found two baby conchs. The snails are still in them, so they'll have to dry a couple weeks on the pier. And this." She holds up a white clay pipe with the longest stem I've ever seen.

"Oh, wow!" Darby says. "Dad is going to go nuts."

"I might not give it to him. I found it. It's mine."

Darby looks at her. "You'd better give it. Don't be stupid."

"You won't tell."

"I will if he asks."

"Come on," I say. "We need to get back before lunch and low tide."

"I'll be there," Sheila waves us off.

*   *   *

Chuck has to tip the little Evinrude into the boat so the blades don't drag. When he and Dad push the boat it squeals against the hard, wet sand. Dad pulls up the little anchor, dripping and trailing black seaweed. He slings it beside Chuck.

"Watch it!" Chuck yells and picks two long strands off his shoulder. He rubs his hands together. "What'd everybody find?"

I turn my hands up. Dad shows his shark's tooth. They're

everywhere. Darby pulls out two arrowheads. One very small and pointy; the other is long and gray.

"When did you find those?" I ask.

"When you weren't looking," she says and hands them to Chuck.

"Ah, these are nice," he says and strokes their edges. Sheila reaches into her bag and shows Chuck the baby conchs.

"Those're going to stink for a good while."

"Anything else in there?" Darby asks.

Sheila looks at her, smiles, and pulls out the broken pipe.

"You broke it! It wasn't broken when she found it. You broke it on purpose!"

"It was already broken when I found it. I just held the stem in place with my hand when I showed it to you." She hands the pieces to Chuck.

"What a beauty. It's a shame these long ones are always busted," he says and throws the pieces overboard.

"You broke it," Darby growls. Sheila just smiles at her.

"Show us yours, Dad."

Chuck pulls out four perfect arrowheads.

"Know what?" Dad says. "I'm thinking of building our own pier. We shouldn't use yours so much."

"True enough."

"Thought I'd ask some of the old-timers at the store for some pointers."

Chuck spits. "They won't help you. You're a foreigner."

"Molly's not. I'm her husband. They should want to help me."

"That doesn't matter. Lisa's been with me fifteen years. Still a foreigner."

"That's ridiculous."

"Way it is. Maybe I'll help you, if I got time."

"Really?"

"We'll see."

Dad gives me a smiley frown. He's pretty pleased with himself. I remind myself not to do anything to spoil his mood. I want us to stay happy.

Everybody falls silent. The nose of the boat bobs and sprays cold mist over us. The sky has darkened weirdly behind us, making the water seem bright.

"You know, I was wondering about Molly." Dad pauses and looks at Chuck. "I mean, she not just confused, you know. And it's not that she's just angry. Something else."

I stare out at the two shrimp trawlers heading our way.

"You know what I mean, Chuck?"

"Not sure I do. She's always had a mean streak. And plenty of imagination."

"That's not quite it."

"You're lettin' her take you for a ride, Nathan."

"Maybe. She's always been high-strung. Ever been anybody else in the family like Molly?"

Chuck's face clamps down on itself. "Nope," he says. "Thank God."

"You sure? I wonder—"

"Hold on," Chuck shouts and cuts the boat across the wake of the trawlers. We grab the sides of the boat. We slam into each wave hard and bounce back up in the air. Darby and Sheila look at each other and scream, their long hair flying up and tangling together.

1976

I know that we are staying at the cottage when Dad decides to build our own pier. It's pretty clear Uncle Chuck doesn't want us to live in the cottage. Mom says it is because he likes to pretend all the land here is his. He won't let me play with Darby and Sheila when he's home; he gives Dad a hard time about the fact that part of the driveway we use is on his property. Chuck even tells me that I can't set one toe on their pier without permission, knowing full well the old one that Grandpa had built decades ago is splintered and wobbly and missing so many planks that to get out to the end is like an elaborate game of hopscotch.

Dad goes to the lumberyard and gets poles and planks and long spiky nails and brings them all down to the water's edge. First he demolishes the old pier. Emma and I sit on shore and watch. The planks aren't a problem, but working the poles up out of the mud is a big job. Uncle Chuck comes out of his house and stands on his pier with his hands on his hips and watches. Then goes back in his house. Half an hour later he comes out again and starts giving my father advice. Then, he does the most shocking thing of all, he strips off his shirt and joins my father in the muck.

Sheila and Darby venture into the yard and we all gather together. Sheila teaches Emma how to make a necklace out of clover. Aunt Lisa brings us food and Darby and I squabble over Pringles. Soon my mother joins us. Sheila runs inside and gets a blanket to spread out. "We're having a September picnic," she sings. Aunt Lisa brings out a bottle of Gallo and soon our mothers are whispering and laughing over their glasses of wine. Darby and I get cans of beer Gan the cooler and Dad and Chuck swim over to drink.

The marsh mud gasps and slurps as they rock and pull the last of the old pier poles out and roll them onshore. Then they install the rest of the poles for the new pier. Dad explains that the poles are too heavy for them to maneuver without the help of the water. My dad grabs a hose and dives down, using the water pressure to blow a hole in the mud, then he and Chuck began working the bottom of the pole into the mud. This goes on and on for hours, our fathers diving into the water, dripping with mud, sunburned purple, as the tide rolls in. As they get more tired and drunk and the water gets higher I am scared my father will drown. When the final pole is ready to go in, they both are tired, and the water has come in to its highest level. As they try to push the last pole in, the bottom flips up out of the water like a shot.

"Son of a bitch!" my father yells and Chuck laughs.

"Jesus!" Aunt Lisa says in a low scary voice and then when we look at her she laughs it off.

Darby looks at me and shrugs, "They're drunk."

"We'll get her," Chuck says. They swivel the thing down again. Both of them grab hold of the top of the pole, using all their weight and strength to push it in. Once it seems to be in the mud aways, my father dives down with the hose. I hold my breath with him. If I don't let it out while he's underwater then everything will be O.K. I become seized with the thought that my father will die down there. That he will drown or be hit in the head with the pole and then drown. Just when I am ready to bust my breath and stand up and scream from pure tension, he surfaces and the men set to rocking the pole into the mud.

When they are done they swim over to Chuck's pier and pull themselves out of the water. They hose the mud off themselves. They are both sunburned on their arms and backs and chests, but their legs are white. I run over and hug my father. His fingers and hands are puckered from so much time in the water.

Uncle Chuck opens the cooler and then slams the top shut. It's empty. "Darby, go get some more beer." We run to the garage and get a six pack out of the refrigerator. Our mothers are still on the blanket; they are curled up facing each other and laughing. They are both smoking and drinking wine. They are happily drunk. Our fathers are happily drunk, too; hands on hips, they look at the pier poles.

"All you got to do tomorrow is plank it up."

"Piece of cake," Dad says.

"Hey," Uncle Chuck says, "let's make a big supper." Darby and I run along the seawall and shake out the crab pots. Lisa and Mom go into the kitchen and thaw out some flounder my uncle caught. The crabs scuttle and scrape against the sides of the steamer and Darby and I like to watch as their bodies go slow and then steam to a bright orange. We shake on lots of Old Bay seasoning. There's corn and tomatoes from Aunt Pearline's garden and Sheila shows Emma how to mix up an angel food cake from a box. Three years old and she can do it almost by herself.

The grown-ups eat and drink at the big glass table in the dining room and we kids eat on the floor in the den. This is the best food ever. And everything feels right. We eat and talk into the night. Our parents mix daiquiris in the blender and move into the living room to laugh. Emma falls asleep on the couch and Darby and Sheila and I go upstairs. There is a giant window in the television room that looks out over the cove and the ocean. We turn off the light so we can look out over the water. A few boats are out, and the red light–topped buoy flashes on and off.

"Let's tell ghost stories," says Darby. "We did it at Girl Scouts before Carlene got kicked out.

Carlene is the local troop leader. She rents a beachhouse a half mile up the road. I'd visited with my cousins before. She sleeps in a hammock, loves Peter Frampton, knows how to macramé plant holders, drives a cool silver Datsun, and has a boyfriend in Newport News who is black. She told us never, ever, to tell our parents because there aren't any black people in Kechotan and our parents might not understand. Carlene is the coolest thing ever.

142

"Why'd she get kicked out?"

"What do you think, dummy? Pot."

Sheila says, "Anyway, I never liked the smell when she smoked. We always had to sit out on her porch so we wouldn't go home smelling like it."

"What happened?"

"The Troop mams caught her. Now she can't do Girl Scouts anymore."

"Here's one that Carlene told us. It's a true story that happened to a friend of hers. See, there was this girl, she was thirteen, and she went to baby-sit for the first time at a family friends' house in the country. They had twin boys and all the girl had to do was to stay in the house with the twins. The mom and dad had already put them down to bed. She's just hanging out, watching TV, when the phone rings. There's a voice on the other end that says, "Go check on the twins.""

"Who is this?" the girl says.

"Go check on the twins," a creepy voice says.

"Darby, stop it," I say. "I don't want to hear about babies dying."

"Would you let me tell the story?"

"I'm serious, I don't want to hear about dead babies!"

"It's O.K., Gingie," Sheila says.

"All right." I cross my arms tight across my chest.

"So the voice says, 'Go check on the twins.' So the girl hangs up the phone. Checks on the babies, and they are fine. She figures it's just a prank call. So she goes back to watching TV. Then the phone rings again."

"Darby, stop, I can't stand it."

"She picks up the phone. 'Go check on the twins. Go check

on the twins.' So she goes and she checks on the twins, and everything is fine. She decides that it is her older brother playing a trick on her.

"Then the phone rings a third time. 'Go check on the twins.' 'You're a dipshit, Jason,' she says, but then there's a knock on the door and it's her brother checking up on her. "In a panic she calls the police and tells them what has happened and that they have to trace the last call to the house. After a few minutes the phone rings again.

"Oh, God!" I scream.

"It's the police. "Get out of the house now, they tell her. The call is coming from *inside the house!*"

I scream and Sheila screams and Darby falls on her back and laughs and laughs.

Sheila tells the next one. "Once there was a woman who lived here when the cows were kept on Cow Island and the bulls on Bull Island. When the tide went out, they'd sometimes bring the cows over to mate with the bulls. Well, one day a woman everybody called Dolly Mama was taking her herd across and began to fill her jumper with oysters she found. They got too heavy and she sank in the mud and drowned. Sometimes, people still see her wandering the marsh."

"Ew!"

"You tell one, Gingie."

I think for a minute, but I don't know any ghost stories at all, other than the story one of the Navy men told me about an old house in Virginia Beach. "Once there was a woman who lived down the street from us who got a horse. She loved this horse so much. She took it riding every day, she brushed it and loved it. Her husband, though, became jealous of the horse and one night after a fight, he went out to the stable and shot it dead."

Sheila gasps. "That's awful."

"The wife was so upset she hung herself from the tree in their front yard. And some nights, you can hear hoofbeats down the pavement, but they always stop right in front of their house!"

"Wow," says Sheila.

Darby starts to sing. "She ran calling Wild-fire! She ran calling Wi-i-ild-fire. She ran calling—"

"Shut up," I yell and throw a pillow at her.

"That's a lame story."

"It is not."

"I think it's tragic," Sheila says.

Darby goes, "O.K., Miss Tragedy, you tell us another one."

"Well," says Sheila, brushing her hair away from her face with her fingertips. "This is a true story that happened here in Kechotan. Aunt Pearline told it to me. It's the story of the running woman. Long ago, when the Indians still lived here too, there was this crazy woman whose family kept her locked up in their house. But she kept getting out and running away. They did everything they could to keep her in the house. They put bolts on all the doors and boarded up the windows, but she kept getting out. They tied her up. But she was like Houdini. She'd always get out and run through the marsh. No one knew why. Then, one night she got out and for too long no one noticed. When they found her the next morning, she was in the marsh, her long hair tangled in the tree roots at the water's edge.

"You mean she drowned?" I ask.

"Her hair trapped her. When the tide came in, she was trapped, like a muskrat in a cage, waiting for high tide."

We all go silent.

"Let's faint!" Darby says.

Sheila crouches down and goes first. Darby and I stand behind her. Sheila blows all the breath out of her body and then refuses to breathe, then, just as she wants to take a breath, she stands up fast and passes out, just like that.

I take a turn. The moment right after I stand and right before I faint is wild; I see spots and colors and then it's like everything skips ahead by a minute and I am on the floor. Then Darby goes. After we're done we all lie together on the floor and look at the stars.

"Sometime I want to faint in a graveyard and then wake up," Darby says.

We all know that Darby swallowed a bottle of iodine when she was eight. Somehow, fainting in a graveyard seems like a bad idea. I want to say this, but I don't know how, so I say nothing at all.

"Hey, want to see something?"

Darby brings out a bunch of magazines that she has taken from the mall and a few old ones that Carlene let her have. Playboy's and Penthouse's and Playgirl's. We lock the door to the den and open the magazines. "Ew!" Sheila screams at a picture of two women wearing nothing but high heels and kissing each other.

We go real quiet as we look through the magazines. I don't look anything like the women in here and I know I never will. They all have huge breasts and long windy hair. Sheila looks sort of like them, because she is so pretty, but Darby and I don't at all. The women in the pictures all look like they have been caught at something, their mouths are always open like they're gasping. One woman is wearing shorts and a halter top and is carrying two shiny buckets of milk from a barn. The milk is spilling out of the pails, and the shorts and top she is wearing don't cover her butt or her boobs. She's looking over her shoulder with that gaspy look on her face.

In the *Penthouse* there's one of a woman who looks like Patty Hearst; she's naked too, except for her blue sunglasses and a pair of handcuffs and chains on her legs. Two policemen are taking her to a jail cell but she doesn't look scared, she looks like she's got a secret. I feel funny looking at these pictures, not just like I am doing something wrong, but liking it too, wanting to see all the pictures. Then I just feel all nasty inside.

The one picture that freaks me out the most is one of a shiny naked woman looking right at me and unzipping her skin. But then I see that it's not her skin she's unzipping but a vinyl body suit that looks like skin and even has breasts and hair. Why would anyone wear such a thing? It is weird. Her clothes make her look naked and she is naked underneath. Or is she?

Darby shows us a *Playgirl* magazine that is full of big-chested men with what looks like the exact same enormous penis over and over and over. These pictures are not as interesting to us as the women. Those pictures we study carefully as if we are studying what it is *Seventeen* says we are supposed to wear on the first day of school. But there's an article in one of the *Playgirl*'s that I read about a woman who sounds like my mother, who is investigating the Watergate hearings, Martha Mitchell, and Patty Hearst. She says that America could turn into Vietnam. I don't know what she means by this—does she think there will be a war in America? I don't understand everything she is talking about, but I begin to wonder if she knows about the secret war. Mostly I think the secret war isn't real, but then I read something like this and I get excited. Maybe it really is real. Maybe Mom is right. Maybe the ghost girl is real, maybe she'll come back. If the world is about to change then I am special: I get to know about it first.

"I'm tired," Sheila says. "Let's go to sleep." She gets up, turns on the bathroom light. "You better hide those from Mom and Dad," she tells Darby. "They'll kill you if they find them." I want to steal the *Playgirl* for the article, but if Mom ever found it, she'd flip. Darby and I take the magazines and go into the attic, where she stuffs them under some insulation. Then we lie on the den floor side by side, Sheila, Darby, me, and we all slip into nothing.

*   *   *

The next morning Dad and I head out to the cove and he nails long planks along the sides of the pier to support the walking planks. Then he nails the walking planks one by one until he is at the very end of our pier and can walk back. Chuck doesn't come out to help this time. And Darby and Sheila are inside cleaning the house with Aunt Lisa. Dad yells at me to go get Mom and Emma so they can come see the pier. I run through the woods to the cottage and tell Mom the pier is done, but she doesn't want to come. She's pacing inside.

"What's wrong?" I ask her.

"Aunt Lisa. She wants honesty and then I give it to her and she can't handle it. Don't ever be like that. Don't ask people for their opinion and then turn into a big whiny baby when it's not what you want to hear."

I want to ask her what she said, what she did, but my stomach twists. If I ask my mother what she did she'll think that I am accusing her of something. So I ask about Aunt Lisa instead.

"What did Aunt Lisa want to know?"

"Oh, she told me she loved me and then asked if I loved her. I thought about it, and I said no. Truth be told, no. And she started crying and said that was a horrible thing to say and ran off to their house."

Last night was wonderful. We were all together and today it's bad again. I want to scream at my mother. I want to know why everything has to turn bad, why she has to ruin everything for me. But I don't. I just leave and go back to the pier.

"Where's your mom?"

"She didn't want to come. She and Aunt Lisa had a fight."

"Aw, Jesus Christ."

"They don't fight about anything that matters."

"Well, they've just never liked each other."

"Why?"

"Sometimes people aren't able to answer that. Your mom and Lisa are like that. Maybe they think if they fight, they can figure out why."

"Maybe." Or maybe they could just shut up and stop ruining everybody else's lives.

Dad and I stand still, looking out at the pier and the sea grass. Dad puts his arm around me. "C'mon," he says and we walk out to the end of the pier. The wood smells sweet and warm. "Not too bad for a first pier," he says.

"I think it looks good."

"At least we won't have to worry about Chuck giving us a hard time about using his pier. Hey, maybe we'll even get a boat." He rubs the top of my head. My head and eyes hurt and I am tired from staying up so late.

"Welp," Dad says as we walk back to the cottage, "at least now we can walk on water, just like everybody else around here."

1977

*A*s my New Year's resolution I decide that since I have no real religion, I will get some. Since I am a blank slate, and I live in a free country, I am free to choose my faith. Since my mother's family was Baptist, when Carol finally asks me what religion we are, it seems O.K. to tell her that I am Baptist but that my father is Episcopalian; because of their differences my parents had stopped attending services. Just like that, Carol invites me to her church, and just like that, I accept the offer. In church I would have Carol all to myself and get to spend some extra time with her. It was perfect.

That weekend I announce to my family my desire to attend Emmaus Baptist Church. My parents are puzzled by my new-found desire for religion and must see that it is based solely on my desire to hang out with Carol Carpenter. I can tell they think that my desire to get religion is a passing fancy, but I don't care what anybody thinks, as long as my father gets up and drives me to Sunday school.

Much like regular school, Sunday school is butt-numbingly dull. I do enjoy reading stories: Job and Esther are my favorites. The classroom itself is small and warm from the radiators that tick on and on from October to April no matter what the temperature outside. The walls are hung with pictures of Jesus on the cross (no blood, just soft dark wounds) in a blue choir robe and a butter yellow glow around his head. In one picture His image is suspended in a bright blue sky over a lush green pasture full of fluffy sheep that looks more like a travel brochure for Ireland than Israel.

His image in the Baptist church is wholly unlike the picture of Christ drawn in Marcella and Marcia Capelletti's Sunday school coloring book, which shows Jesus looking like He walked out of a concentration camp and then got hoisted onto the cross like a tattered flag. On the cover of the coloring book blood drips from His body and His head and His thorny crown lists to the side.

In the Baptist church Jesus looks nice; he never appears scary and naked and dead. The Capellettis tell us about Mass, which we understand as the same boring church service every week, or every day if you are like their grandmother. Worst of all, we are thrilled and appalled to hear of the unsanitary habits of the Catholics. Baptists and Methodists would never in a million years drink from the same cup and have the minister wipe the spit off. Everyone knows you can get really sick doing a thing like that! Communion time at Emmaus Baptist is kind of like fancy snacktime at kindergarten—two giant silver trays, one with individual little bread squares and another that holds fifty separate shot glasses full of Welch's grape juice.

None of us have ever seen anything like the Catholic Christ, and then Lisa Gilmore, the only girl in the school who can really draw a horse, says when she was over the Capellettis' house that they all had similarly grisly crucifixes over the beds and doorways. Our entire homeroom is scandalized but completely fascinated, and I am teeth-gnashing jealous of the Capelletti twins' rise in popularity.

When *The Exorcist* comes out we grill them shamelessly about demon possession and asked if they have ever witnessed an exorcism. They laugh and wave their hands dismissively until finally one afternoon, they convince Melinda Murphy that she is possessed of a minor demon and that any Catholic is allowed to perform an exorcism.

Miss Alexander gets wind of it at recess just as we have undone the laces of Melinda's shoes to tie her hands so she won't hurt herself when her demon emerges. Miss Alexander sits us all down and declares that, "Miss Alexander will be calling parents." She explains that only a priest can perform an exorcism and that anyway they are utter hogwash. "Miss Alexander will tell you what is real. What is real is excommunication, which is when the pope throws naughty Catholic girls out of the Church so that they will burn in hell. Maybe Miss Alexander will just go ahead and write a little letter to the pope letting him know what the Cappelletti girls have been up to? Hmmm. What do you think of that?" Everyone is terrified except Marcella and Marcia, who roll their eyes and tell us that they will light a candle each for Miss Alexander and her stupidity.

On the way home from school I tell Carol that Aunt Lisa thinks my Man should set exercised because she's been acting

so stange. "Wouldn't work, she says." "You have to be Catholic
to be posessed." "Do you think Miss Alexander can really get
the Capelletti's thrown out of the Catholic Church?" I ask
Carol. She is unclear on this point. She says it will be hard—
Catholics confess their sins each week and are then forgiven.
Marcella and Marcia are probably safe from hell, unless they
forget to tell something at confession, and then she guesses
they could confess it later and be forgiven for both the sin and
the forgetting.

"It's different with Baptists," she explains. "You have to be
saved. You know, born again." After school that afternoon she
shows me her baptism dress, a beautiful floor-length waterfall
of blue satin and lace. We sit in her closet and run our hands
up and down the cool slick fabric.

Everyone goes to church except me. And if I become a
member of the Baptist church I will get a new dress and a new
life and Carol Carpenter as my best friend. I immediately decide that I must be saved too. "How do you do it?" I ask her.
"How do you get saved?"

Carol explains that to be saved from hell you have to be
baptized. And that once you are baptized and accept Jesus
Christ as your Lord and personal savior you are born again.
Washed. Pure. New. "On Sundays, Reverend Dewberry always
asks who wants to accept Jesus into their hearts and sometimes folks go up. That means that they'll get baptized a few
weeks later.

All I can think about after that is how much I want to be
baptized. I don't tell anyone of my wish. Keeping my desire a
secret makes it stronger. After two weeks, the urge is still there

and I know. I make up my mind on Sunday morning—when I go to the church service and Reverend Dewberry asks if anyone there would like to accept Jesus Christ into their heart as their Lord and personal savior—I will rise out of my pew to walk to the front of the church and declare my love for Christ.

But when the time comes for me to walk up front, I am terrified. I tell myself that no one will see me if I trip since everyone has their eyes closed. So I rise from my pew, my face aflame; my legs have the feeling scared right out of them. As I make my way up to the altar I cling to the edges of the pews, convinced that everyone is snoozing under their hats or praying so hard for folks like me to be saved by Jesus Christ that I muster the courage to make it all the way to the front. For two weeks I have held this secret in my heart. I will be changed. I will be transformed. I will become a member of the church. I will be saved by Jesus Christ and rescued. He will love me. I believe that I will be made worthy, not only in the eyes of the people in the church, who will somehow view my family with more sympathy, but by Carol, who will begin to think of me as her sister. We will be best friends.

After church that afternoon I tell my parents that I have accepted Jesus as my savior and that I will be baptized.

"What?"

"Baptized. I'm going to be a member of Emmaus. Reverend Dewberry will be coming out to talk to you all about it since you're not members."

"Jesus Christ, Virginia!" Mother says and laughs.

"Molly, c'mon."

My father sits down beside me. "Are you sure that you

want to be baptized? Is this really what you believe? That Jesus died for your sins? Do you really understand and believe what Emmaus teaches? If you do, that's fine. This is your decision. But this is serious, O.K.?"

I nod. I'm not sure at all what I believe about the Church, but I have faith in Carol. I know that I have love and hope and believe in God and Jesus enough and figure becoming a member of the Church will help me understand these things better. I believe enough not to back out of the deal.

"This is what I want," I tell my father.

Then my parents shock me and do the most unexpected thing: They hug me and tell me they are proud of me. I am making my own decisions. Growing up. My mother has tears in her eyes. She says they are tears of joy.

*   *   *

In two weeks I will be baptized and everything will be better. I won't feel bad anymore. My family will be somehow healed. I will work hard in school and make good grades. We will live the way I imagine all good families do. My mother drives me to Penney's in Newport News and we buy a beautiful full-length dotted-Swiss pink granny dress with a bit of lace on the hem and on the sleeves. My arms are just a bit too big for the sleeves, but I get the dress anyway, even though the elastic leaves two red dented bracelets on my flesh.

On the evening of my baptism I am excited. I peek from behind the altar as the church fills up. My whole family comes together, even my grandfather and step-grandmother from Newport News, who was born again in the Baptist church fifteen years earlier, to watch me.

There's not been a time in the history of our family that everyone has come together like this that I can recall and I feel powerful. It is an event with a capital E. One of the church ladies leads me upstairs into the ladies' dressing area. There's one for the men on the other side and each dressing room has separate steps in and out of the font. I imagine myself up in the baptismal font being dipped in the water and emerging reborn. I will be a born-again Christian, just like Eric Clapton. I imagine myself free, liberated. I will be a child of God. I will be saved. The cold and misery in my chest and guts will be replaced with the light of the Lord, and my life will be changed. I have let Jesus into my heart and I do feel Him knocking around inside me. But my desire is deeper. My desire is to be infused. My burdens will be lifted, given up to the Lord. The church lady leads me to the steps that descend into the font and taps my shoulder when it's time. I'm first in line, then a gray-haired man who is getting baptized for the first time too.

The baptismal font is filled like a bathtub. Reverend Dewberry steps in first and his black robe flows around his knees like a pool of ink. His feet are bare, and his pants are cuffed up above his knees. He has ringworm on the top of his foot, a small pink stamped hollow O the size of a nickel and I think that I don't want to step in the same water as him, but it is too late, and besides, what sort of god would let me get ringworm from my preacher on the day of my baptism? I am offstage at the top of the steps, and he motions me down. In front of what feels like the whole world, I walk out to Reverend Dewberry. In the water, my dress bloats out all humpy around my legs and belly but since it isn't a swirly dance dress, it doesn't slide up high enough to reveal more than my

157

knees. The light in the font shines down from a frosted globe whose wire laces through its chain and anchors in the center of the arched ceiling. The water is clear, plain water—there's even a round slotted steel drain in the floor of the font and a spigot on the side. When I imagined the water up here it was the deep blue of the river in the baptismal mural that now, up close, looks fakey, like one of those paint-by-number sets that only seems real when it's far enough away that your eye can blend it together.

Reverend Dewberry says a few words and then asks me if I am prepared to accept Jesus Christ into my heart as my sole and personal savior.

I say yessir and then he drops opens his white handkerchief to cover his hand as he pinches my nose shut tight. I take hold of his forearm and he tips me back into the bathwater and then holds me under. I can hear him saying something and I open my eyes and see his choppy face, the bleary globe of light suspended from the ceiling of the font, and the slithering river in the baptismal mural. My chest starts to burn with my last breath and I wonder is this the spirit of God, burning out what is impure and scouring me clean for my new life? When Reverend Dewberry pulls me up, I am elated and gasping and the blue silky curtain that covers the font closes. He smiles and walks out the men's side of the font. I walk up the stairs of the ladies', expecting to be flying, but I'm soaking wet and having a hard time even moving in the heavy dress. It keeps sticking to my thighs and slurps as I try to pull it away from my skin. Slick and goose-pimpled, I shuck off my pretty dress and the church lady in the dressing room hangs it to drip dry on a little clothesline. I reach into the Richfood bag for my Toughskins and a turtleneck to wear to the potluck supper. When I look in the dressing room mirror I am ashamed. Nothing has changed. I feel so disappointed and terribly alone. I may have been born again, but right then I knew that though God might love me and I might love Him, and that He might be able to save my soul, He wasn't going to rescue me. That was my job.

1977

February starts out cold and rainy. The rain isn't strong but it is steady for nearly two full weeks and everywhere we walk at school and home is puddled and muddy. The wheel wells of our car are splattered and caked with large clots of mud. Every morning I hear the tires on my father's Maverick spin and spit through the mud down the old grassy drive. One morning I listen as the engine revs and revs. He slams the door and comes back into the cottage.

"Get your shoes on, Molly. I need your help."

The grassy drive from our cottage to the road is torn up, the Maverick's wheels are sunk deep into the mud. Dad gets Mom to sit in the front seat and gun the engine while he stands behind the car and tries to rock the car out of the groove. I am on the side of the drive. The car door is open and I watch my mother's mud and pine-needle-caked slipper push the pedal as my father tries to rock the car forward. The car revs and whines and the back wheels carve out sloppy gullies. I worry that my mother is going to rev the engine and run over my father while he is under the back tire or that a board will shoot out and take off his head. But the car just sinks until the wheels are barely visible. My mother gets out of the car, and her slippers vanish in the soft mud. Clearly she thinks this is hilarious, because she just laughs and laughs.

My father glares at her. His face goes red trying to contain his frustration and rage. His shoes and pants are ruined in the filth. Tiny mud droplets bead on his face and eyelashes and stain his tie in little streaks that look like a rain shower. Mom's laughter is mean. Can't she see that my father is furious. Can't she see how hard he is working when she does nothing, nothing at all?

"Stop it!!!" I scream out of sheer tension.

Emma watches us from behind the screen door.

My mother keeps laughing, tears spilling down her face.

My father hangs his head and breathes like a bull, the way he does when he's trying hard not to yell. "Get in the goddamned house, Molly," he growls at her. "If you're not going to help, just go away."

My mother puts her hand on her hip and opens her mouth and I think I will just die on the spot, but then she clamps her mouth shut tight, turns, and slogs back up to the cottage. She slams the door behind her.

"Can you get behind the wheel?" Dad asks me.

I nod. I slide in the Maverick, and Dad scootches the seat up far enough so my toes can press the pedals.

"O.K., stop!!" my father yells. "Go!" My father jams more two by fours under the tires to get some traction. He sets them under and then stands to the side. He grabs my shoulder through the window. "Don't touch that pedal until I'm beside you and tell you to go. Got it. I don't want one of the boards to fly and take me out." But the boards he jams under the tires just sink into the mud; there isn't even enough traction to push them out. He puts a flattened cardboard box and more boards on top of that, but the car just sinks in deeper. He finally comes over and bangs on the window.

"There's so much water, it's impossible."

"We can call a tow truck, Daddy."

"No. Tow truck would sink too. We're just going to have to leave it and wait."

Blue Heron sends a company car for Dad to use and he parks it on the street. He walks up the long muddy driveway each day for a week, past the stuck car. Then a sudden hard freeze descends, and the temperatures fall into the single digits. No one here, not even the old-timers can recall such cold. The world seizes up. The saltwater inlets freeze. The piers in town rise and curl back toward shore. The Maverick is clenched tight in its pit. Worst of all we are all stuck together in the drafty cottage. We gather around the space heater. Emma and I huddle in tents we make out of blankets. I read books. Dad and Mom wear their coats in the house and are painfully quiet on the weekend. Mom escapes the tension in the house by sleeping, and Dad watches football.

The cold makes everything sound so loud. The wind in the branches overhead, our voices, the planes from Langley. The freeze lasts ten days at most, but it seems longer. When my father and I walk past the Maverick to get the newspaper one morning he yells at the sky, "O.K., I get it. We're stuck in this shithole. Now would you turn up the goddamn heat?"

1977

A week or so after the freeze finally ends, I am waiting alone at the school bus stop when my father drives up. I'd left the cottage early because he and my mother were fighting and I had to get out. Nothing outside seems as bad as inside that cottage.

My father is crying and he leans out of the car window to give me a hug.

"What's wrong?"

He sighs; it's a heavy and mournful sound.

"Your mother and I are getting a divorce," he says. "I am going to find someplace to live. I don't know what to say. I'm sorry, sweetie."

I look in the back of car and see his suitcase and kit bag. He's really leaving. He's leaving me.

"I want to come with you," I tell him.

"You can't. The mother usually gets the kids, but we'll work out custody. I'll have to talk to a lawyer. Anyway, we'll

talk about this later. I just want you to know that I love you
and that I am sorry."

I can't speak, so I hug him through the car window and
watch him drive off. Just like that the world has changed. I
take Miss Ruth's star out of my back pocket and look at it. I
think of it as a lucky compass. I slip it back in my pants.

Suddenly everything feels spongy. The street. My face. My
insides. Then I have a thought: I am not going to go to school
today. I think about walking home, but I don't. There's no
place I want to go. I ditch my book bag under a bayberry tree
and walk up the street. When I see the school bus, I hide until it passes.

I walk by Miss Ruth's house. It's Wednesday, her cleaning
day, and her kitchen and pantry windows are open and I can
smell the Pine-Sol clear out to the street. When I look through
the glass of her kitchen door she is on her knees, scrubbing
the floors. I wave and she lets me in. She has her yellow rubber gloves on and her cleaning apron, a bibbed affair covered
with faded zinnias and neatly repaired pockets on each hip.

She gives me a long look. I am scared that she will ask me
what I am doing here and how come I am not in school but
instead she starts scrubbing again.

"Get a brush, Grinchie!"

I did as I was told. I dip the wooden scrub brush into the
bucket and my hands go warm as soon as the bleach water
touches them. I love the smell of bleach. It reminds me of my
father and of our laundry room in Virginia Beach, and how
when we lived there my father's undershirts smelled mildly
caustic, how he stacked them in tight little packages ready to

go into his dresser. Now that we live in the cottage everything smells like mildew.

I can't smell this bleach without smelling all the smells of my father—his Prell shampoo, his deodorant, his shaving cream and aftershave, gin and tonics, Desitin and baby oil, mother's Kents, and her Windsong perfume—a heady mixed-up warm and cool smell that is his scratchy face kissing me good-bye.

I scrub the kitchen with Miss Ruth in silence. We scrub her counters, clean out her cabinets and wipe them down, empty and wash down her refrigerator, even her cabinet doors. Once we pour out the gray water, I feel scrubbed out myself. All the darkness that had collected in my chest and mind like old wet leaves and lint is gone and in its place is something fresh like a clean red-rimmed enamel metal bowl or Emma's cool damp hand after we bathe side-by-side in the kitchen sink in the cottage, Emma in the shallow sink and me, long legs and arms folded up like a Japanese paper bird, in the deep sink beside her.

Miss Ruth feeds me lunch and we sit on her porch while I play with Ashes. Then she takes a nap. Later, we watch *Days of Our Lives* and *General Hospital* and eat vanilla ice cream out of custard dishes. She must know that I am skipping school but doesn't look up at me when the school bus drives past to drop off the kids.

"I'll wash these," I tell her and take our dishes to the kitchen sink. I wash them out, but can't find a dish towel. "I need a dishcloth," I call.

"In the buffet."

I go into the dining room and open the drawer to the buffet. Miss Ruth's Christmas stars are collected there, on top of a neatly stacked pile of dish towels. I reach into my pocket. I should never have taken my North Star from Miss Ruth.

I look up and Miss Ruth is right there, looking at me. I feel an electric shock go down my arms

"What's this?" she says.

I think I might faint from fear. I can't speak.

"What's that in your pocket? Go on, show me, girl."

She thinks that I am stealing from her again. But I am not stealing, I am returning. But I have stolen from her and she knows it and she wants to catch me at it. And I am caught. I love Miss Ruth. But I want to die from my shame and embarrassment.

I pull the star out of my pocket and set it on top of the buffet.

"Oh, dear," she says. "I'm very disappointed." I nod and run out of her house.

I run all the way home. I plan on going to my room and hiding in bed. I'll tell my mother I am sick. But when I get there, there's Dad's car and Dad is home. He's not going to leave. He's going to stay. I know I should feel happy and grateful, but I don't. I just feel tired.

1977

*O*ne weekend afternoon in a fit of boredom and bravery, I walk to Sheila and Darby's to see if they want to play, but they have gone away for a weekend at band camp in Hampton Roads. "You could try Carol's," my aunt suggests. But Carol's gone with her parents to West Virginia. "It's O.K." I tell my aunt and uncle. "I'll just go exploring by myself."

"Yep," my uncle says, "it's why I like going out fishing alone. Hell is other people." He sticks his hands deep in his pockets and walks down the stairs to his workshop. My aunt stares at back at him, surprised. "Some people are hell," she whispers, then she looks at me. "But some are heaven."

I have no idea what to believe.

1977

*I*t is Spring time and my father begins jogging. He's slow at first. His plain white tennis shoes offer no buffer for his feet striking the pavement and leave him rattled from toes to teeth with pain. He takes off from the end of our driveway, but can only make it a quarter mile up our road and returns, walking, hands on his hips, and stooped forward, winded, nearly convulsed. He leans against our mailbox until he catches his breath. "I ran miles each day in the Army with a pack and combat boots, and I can't even make it the half mile around the goddamned block."

He gets a pair of real Adidas running shoes, aptly named Country Runners, and slowly works his way to three miles a day, then six. He loses his fat and becomes lean and stringy; his jowls vanish and his cheeks hollow and sharpen to the point where people ask if he's well. "The world is overweight," he tells me. "If somebody tells you you look healthy, you know you need to lose a few." Soon there's no place for me to rest my head on his arms or belly.

I love to see Dad run; he's like a deer, but it kills me to see him disappear. On jogging days, I watch from the end of the driveway as he glides away, Ralph running alongside, until he becomes small enough to hold on my fingertips and then is swallowed into the long tarry blur of road. One day when he returns I tell him that I worry when he runs that he won't come back. He rubs my head and puts his hands on his knees. "I'm here. You worry too much." This is not what I want to hear.

"Hey, do you know Zeno's paradox? A long time ago there was a man named Zeno. He said if you try to run a hundred miles, you first have to run half of it. Then you have fifty miles to go. So you run half of that—twenty five miles. Then half of twenty-five, then half of twelve and a half. And so on. The runner always has half the distance left to cover. So how is it possible to finish?" This is not the answer I am looking for. It's no sort of answer at all.

I watch the clock when I am at school. A class is an hour. Once I have endured thirty minutes, I only have another thirty to go. First I have to get through the next fifteen. Then the next seven and a half. I keep going, but the bell always rings and the class ends.

Things end. Races, classes, books. I decide I hate Zeno and all people who play games with words and figures to make themselves look smart.

But now when Dad runs and vanishes into the road I hug myself tight and climb up the wild cherry tree to hide. I think about being left. I think that Dad is running because he wants to run away from us and that every time he has to turn around to come home he would rather keep running. I more than think this, I know this, because it is exactly the same way I feel when I come home from school or Carol Carpenters'. One day, I have promised myself, it is exactly what I will do—leave, evaporate into nothing like a foggy morning. I just don't want him leaving before I do.

I create my own daytime nightmares about this, terribly vivid and detailed. When I do this at first it seems a way that makes it O.K. for me to be so scared and teary. But then I can't stop thinking this way until he gets back and I am so elated to have him return that I fling myself against him until my fear leaves me the next day. Soon my nightmare fantasy changes: My father is killed by a car and the police come to the cottage to tell us. My mother is despondent, Emma howls, but I can't get upset. I try to make myself cry, but there's nothing in me anymore that feels alive. I'm somewhere else, I'm in a silent pool of water, floating beneath the surface, I'm in the rafters looking down, I'm a cloud or a leaf.

The more I think like this the more real my fantasy becomes. Each time I make Dad die I tell myself that we will be fine. We have everything we need here to survive.

Mother, Emma, and I will lead a life that's some sort of cross between *Little Women* and *Little House on the Prairie*. Some days I try to stop myself from thinking this way, worried that these daydreams mean I want my father to die.

Mostly, though, thinking like this eases some pressure in me. Soon, I learn that I can disappear anytime I like, and without running away—I relax my eyes so my world goes double and then blurs into a haze. I create car crashes and drownings and shipwrecks. I cover us all in hot lava, I start an avalanche, I make planes fall from the sky. I'm a tidal wave, a tornado, an earthquake. I don't have to be scared—I've already made the worst things happen.

1977

A month before school lets out the pines swell with pollen and release it until a sulfur-yellow dust coats every outdoor surface from planter to doorknob, porch and windshield. Though it seems to have rained all winter long and we prayed for it to stop, now it is unbearably dry. Breathing the air is like walking through a powder puff. The sky stays a constant swimming-pool blue until school lets out for vacation and summer arrives. So little rain has left the edges of the marsh crazed with cracks.

There is nothing to do in Kechotan in the summertime. After my father and uncle have gone off to work, Aunt Lisa cleans the house, does the laundry, and begins preparing the meals for the day. My mother stays up late and sleeps in late. Emma and I watch the little black-and-white TV in the mornings and play outside. When Mom wakes up at midday she smokes and writes in her notebooks, which worries me, because it means she is still thinking about the war.

One afternoon, when my mother is sunbathing on our pier and we girls are skipping rocks by the landing, Aunt Lisa calls from their pier that Mom should come over and have a glass of wine. All of us hold our breath, waiting to see what my mother will say, but to my shock, and to Lisa's and Darby's too, Mom stands up, wraps the towel around her waist, and says, "I wouldn't mind that one iota." After that we see our mothers together again in the afternoons, sitting on the edge of the seawall or dock drinking a beer or a glass of wine in the long afternoon hours before the men come home. I think for a while that they are really making up, but I begin to see that they are as bored and lonely as we girls are. They are the only young mothers nearby."

While our mothers are outside, Sheila, Darby, and I play in the house. In one of Aunt Lisa's magazines I read a story about how Patty Hearst had been locked in a closet for over a month and that is why she went over to the SLA. They brainwashed her. I am not sure that I believe in brainwashing. Lots of people aren't sure, says the article. That's why Patty was found guilty, because people weren't sure what to think.

There are pictures of her. In one Patty looks happy in handcuffs, in another her fist is held high in the air. In another, though, she looks tired and broken.

I wonder what it would be like to be in a closet for over a month. So I go into Darby's room and step into the closet and close the door behind me. Inside her closet is another world. The world of fancy studded bell-bottom pants, of a poster of Elton John on the interior door. Of her tennis shoes and church shoes and strange shiny patent leather platforms that she wore to a clarinet recital at school. Aunt Lisa made her wear a girdle too, because she said Darby was getting fat.

I turn off the light. At first it is pitch black. Then I begin to focus on the light that comes in from the outside. Soon, my eyes adjust and I begin to see the shapes of things around me. The drape of a coat, the crumpled T-shirt in a corner. I see the knot in the wood grain of the shelf over my head. I am all alone. Soon, I am bored. And I have only been in the closet for five minutes. Not five weeks. I hear the front door slam. Sheila and Darby have gone outside to play

I ask myself: *Don't you wish that you could have gone outside? Aren't you sad that you had to spend all your time in a yucky closet while they have snail races outside on the pier?*

I say: No.

I say to myself in my best kidnapper voice: *What did you say?*

I say: Nothing.

I say to myself: *What?*

I say: (Silence.)

I say to myself: *That's better.*

Now if you do not wish to stay my prisoner you will have to learn to do as I say. Do you understand? Otherwise we will just leave you in the closet.

I say: *I don't care.*

Though really what I mean is that I am ready to be transformed. I am ready to have a new experience and to be utterly and completely changed. I am ready to assume my new identity.

I want to rob a bank. I want to steal things from people. I want to be a stowaway on an airplane. I want to participate in a skyjacking.

When I walk out of the closet, I imagine I will be a different person, but when I step out into Darby's room, my eyes swim in the light and then I am just Gingie again.

*   *   *

I go outside. Mom and Aunt Lisa are still drinking on the pier and Sheila and Darby are outside catching ladybugs near the landing.

"Hey," they say.

I think I will see if I am tougher from my experience in the closet. "Cram it," I tell them and they laugh.

"So what do you all want to do?" I ask.

"Let's play kick the can," says Sheila. So we do.

1977

*M*uch of that spring and summer I spend at Carol's house. We're best friends; we even cut our thumbs and bind them together like Indians. After church I go back to the Carpenters' to have a sandwich and play with their dog, Foxy, who looks to be part border collie and part golden retriever, with a little bit of German shepherd tossed in. "Daddy says she's just like us—an all-American mutt." Foxy has just given birth to a litter of six pups. Mr. Carpenter lets Carol keep them in his garage, a filthy jumble of old tractor parts, rusted toys from Carol and her three grown sisters, and what looks like at least a hundred bottomless lawn chairs. Nothing stored there looks like it will ever be used again, but Carol says he can't bear throwing anything away.

The Carpenters' garage is cool and dank and smells sweetly of piss and motor oil. Foxy lies in the corner, on a dingy pink blanket, her babies cuddling next to her. Carol and I press our shins against the cool cement floor and scoop the pups into our hands. They are warm and soft and slack as dough. Some have yet to open their eyes and are all mouth and bright sharp teeth—Carol shows me how to slip a pinky in so they'll suck.

We hold the pups close to our chests as if they are our babies, rub our noses against theirs, nuzzle their fuzzed fat bodies. When the pups are hungry, they whine and whimper and jockey for a place on Foxy's long gray teats.

"Do you want one?" Carol asks. "You can have your pick of the litter."

"We already have Ralph. I don't think I can get another dog."

She holds up an orange-and-white-spotted pup with a white ring around her nose and little white feet. "This is Cupcake. She's my favorite. I'm gonna ask Daddy if I can keep her out of the sack."

I picture Mr. Carpenter' briefly as Santa Claus but I know what she means is that he kills the pups she can't give away.

"You could get Foxy fixed so she wouldn't have any more puppies."

"It's too expensive. And I like her having puppies. It's fun."

Until they get sacked, I think. "How many babies has she had?"

"This is her seventh batch."

"And all of them wind up—"

"No. Not all of them. Oncet I gave away all the puppies in the litter except the runt."

I don't know how Carol can stand it. I'd been upset this past summer when my mother set out dog food with paint stripper on it for the moles. The poor blind things crawled out of their holes with their innards tumbling from their mouths. Puppies are another deal altogether.

I ask my parents if I can have one of the puppies and they say no. I beg.

"But Mr. Carpenter will kill them."

"That man sure as hell should have that dog spayed."

"Ralph's not fixed."

"Ralph's a boy," my father says. "He's not bringing home puppies."

"Those could be Ralph's puppies."

"Virginia—"

"We have to find homes for the puppies."

"Not this home."

"Then we have to get Foxy spayed so she won't have any more puppies!"

"Look, Gingie," my father says. "The guy's a jerk for not spaying the dog and then killing the puppies he can't give away, only to have it all happen again. It's not too expensive. But it's not our business. You need to butt out."

I refuse to quit. Carol and I hang little signs at school and church and tell all of our neighborhood friends. As soon as the puppies start wanting dog food, Carol says, their time is up.

A month or so later no one, not one person, has offered to take any of the dogs. They have grown louder and hop about and wrestle each other. They are now eating dog food mixed with milk and the smell in the garage has soured and thickened. The food bowls are crusted brown around the rim with old Mighty Dog dog food and the new food is crawling with flies.

Carol tells me that today is the day. I think I should leave, but Carol asks me if I can stay. So I do. I don't know what I think I can accomplish by being here or if I think maybe my presence will change Mr. Carpenter' mind or shame him into keeping the puppies. Or maybe I am simply curious.

We load the puppies into a basket and carry them out to Mr. Carpenter's truck and then hop in the back. He drives us through their woods to the boat landing. We get out, and Carol and I start to play with the pups. We've named them all. Mr. Carpenter puts five stones in the bottom of the sack and tells Carol to put the pups in the bag. She loads them in one by one, not holding on to Cupcake any longer than the others. I want to grab one and run home.

The bag bounces and barks and wobbles on the dock and Carol and I laugh at the way it wiggles like Jell-O. Mr. Carpenter ties the top off good and tight and then ties one end of the rope to the pier post and the other to the top of the sack. Then he casts the bag of pups into the water and it sinks with a hiss of bubbles like he's tossing out a crab pot.

"C'mon," Carol says and we walk away. We both go real quiet and a strange thickness descends on everything. I feel like I should be upset, but I am not. I just feel strange and slow. Carol and I play sea captain in the graveyard of fishing boats near the landing, but neither of us has the heart for it. We take turns with the wheel, but right now the game we love feels like a chore, not fun.

Over by the dock, Mr. Carpenter starts pulling the rope in. We walk over to watch. The bag hits the dock so hard it shakes the planks under our feet. I'm startled—I can't help but think that the puppies might get hurt in there. He slits the bag open with his barlow knife and we pull the fabric away to look at the puppies. Mr. Carpenter wants to make sure they are all dead before he buries them. Carol and I just want to see them. Say good-bye again. The puppies are piled all over each other, their fur slicked together. It's hard to tell one from another, all jumbled together and wet like that. One puppy's ear is twisted inside out against its head. It's as pink as a tongue. I want to pick it up but I follow Carol's lead. She stares in the sack and then takes off her flip-flop. With one toe, she nudges Cupcake but gets no response. She takes off her other flip-flop and threads her hands through the thong.

"We're gonna walk back, Daddy," she calls. Mr. Carpenter gets his shovel from the truck bed and begins to dig, the blade screeching in the sand as he prepares the grave.

I begin to understand that Carol doesn't have it as great as I thought.

2000

Memory is a strange thing. As is the lack of it. We were at the cottage for over three years and in all that time I don't remember one birthday of mine or my sister's. I don't remember one Christmas morning, though I do recall cutting down a cedar with my father and carrying it into the cottage. Perhaps I could jog my memory with photographs of these events, but there aren't any. Documentation of our family life stopped in 1975 and resumed only sporadically once we moved to Fairfield. We did our best to erase those years from our lives, even as we were living them.

Part Two

Fairfield, Virginia

2000

*O*ur departure from the cottage in 1978 seemed almost as sudden as our arrival. My father announced that he was taking a job at a bank in Fairfield, near Richmond, Virginia. My mother was furious. She refused to go. My father, in a moment of deep strength, said calmly that she could stay at the cottage if she wished, that he hoped she wouldn't. He was going to take us girls, work in Fairfield, and what she wanted to do was her own goddamned choice. He was calling her bluff. And it worked. She gave in. It surprised me and I think it surprised Dad too, but it also pleased him. He was back in charge. He was feeling strong from running and from finally selling some big commercial properties for the real estate company. He was going to return to his career in banking, buy us a decent house, and get us out.

Our house in Fairfield was lovely. A white house with black shutters and a bright red door. A front and backyard with grass. Two bathrooms and two bathtubs! My own room. My mother redecorated. Lime green carpet was taken up and re-placed with a rust-colored carpet. She repainted rooms and rearranged furniture. But something had changed in my mother that I couldn't quite describe. She had gone flat as if someone had snatched the soul out of her.

That August before school started my father decided that we should all have a real vacation. We rented a hotel room in Virginia Beach and drove down for the week. My mother lay on the sand and stared at the sky. She was too quiet and no matter what we did to try to bring her out, her mouth just smiled her distant smile, but her eyes were somewhere else.

I was on the little hotel balcony when I heard my mother talking and laughing. I went in the room, but there was no-body there. My father was down the hall getting ice. I knew what was happening right then: My mother was hallucinat-ing; she was talking back to the voices she heard in her head. I stepped back out on the balcony. Emma was out there with me, dangling her legs through the iron railing, looking down at the boys doing flips off the pool diving board. I heard my father come back in the room. I heard them talking, my father sounding upset and scared, my mother angry. Emma started to cry, listening to them, and I started to cry watching Emma cry. We could feel it happening again as acutely as a physical pain. I sat down beside Emma and we looked through the balcony bars at the pool. Beyond it was the beach, and beyond the beach the water and then the horizon and then other side of the world, which is where we longed to be.

2000

*F*or many years I blamed my father, blamed him because I thought he could and should rescue us from my mother. Because I thought my mother was the "bad guy." But once she began talking back to the voices in her head he explained to me how sick she was. He began consulting doctors and lawyers and trying to see how to get her help. It was at this point that both he and I began to understand that even if anyone had tried earlier to get my mother help it would have made no difference. She couldn't even get a psychiatric evaluation unless she was suicidal or homicidal. Actually that isn't exactly true—we could only get her a psychiatric evaluation if she "acted on" a suicidal or homicidal impulse and we could prove it with physical evidence. This meant that she had to literally wound herself or someone else. That was the law.

My father's choice was simple and brutal: He could stay and try to help her and honor his vows—after all "in sickness" was part of the deal—or he could abandon her. He chose to stay and tried to talk her into help. For years I hated him for it. And for those same years I respected him and admired him for staying. My father was willing to sacrifice himself for all of us. And he wasn't willing to sacrifice my mother for us or us for her. Finally, a year and a half after we moved to Fairfield, he talked my mother into seeing a doctor, who then hospitalized her. She'd been psychotic for over five years.

1981

*W*hat my sister saw.

"I'll never get out of here," my mother gasps to my father and then calms her voice to a whisper. "I never will." She's been voluntarily committed to the hospital for two weeks of what will be a four-week stay. Her exotic, black hair is pulled back with a two-week-old, ink-stained rubber band from the newspaper, and the lack of style makes her face look flat and tight. But she's found some red lipstick, or a pastel crayon, and has made an attempt at presentability. She holds both her hands close to her chest, as if she is about to pray or defend herself. They tremble so: from too much Lithium, Prolyxin, Haldol? Or plain cold fear?

My father's hands shake too. His hands belong on a work-ingman, not on a man who spends his days at a bank. His heart knows this too, even if he does not. When there's time, or too much time, his hands are often building: a brick patio, a loft; sometimes a chisel turns stone into art or spins clay into bowls. My father looks at my mother's hands as if he may press them to his cheek, but instead he just squeezes them tight between his own as if to say: I can protect you. I'm here.

"Of course, you'll get out of here," he scolds her. "Don't talk like that."

My mother slips her hands from his and encircles herself with her arms. "I'm cold, Nathan. You're sweet for coming." She hugs my six-year-old sister and gives her a tight wistful look. "See you soon, Emma Byrd." Then she turns toward the safety of the ward. "Wait here," my father tells my sister, wide-eyed on the hospital bench. "Don't you talk to anyone."

He goes after my mother, pulls off his old black-and-tan plaid wool jacket, puts it over her shoulders, and spins her around. He waves to my sister to get up.

My mother gasps, horrified. When she sees my father's impish face, she smiles, and flashes the gap between her front teeth. "Nathan," she scolds him. "What on earth are you do-ing?"

He nuzzles her cheek. "We're leaving. I want an ice cream."

They head down the hallway, past the nurses' station and the residents, toward the red beacon of the exit sign.

"Nathan?" My mother's gait has slowed and she's taking breaths like little sobs.

"Hey, hey. It's just for an ice cream. Pistachio. You need to get out. We'll be right back, O.K.?" He winks one blue eye at her and then slips his red freckled hand up her sleeve to hide her hospital ID bracelet. "They'll never even know you were gone."

My mother takes my father's proffered arm and they hurry the pace. My sister is sweaty with excitement, my father full of purpose and disdain. My mother uncurls herself a bit, her chin up, a sense of freedom restored. They march past a hospital full of official white-shod employees, ride down the escalator, stroll through the lobby. Then they push through the exit doors of the Medical College of Virginia Hospital and walk out, just like anybody else.

2000

I never visited my mother in the hospital. I was so happy she was gone. When I came home from school I could walk in the house and breathe. I didn't have to worry about where my mother was or doing something to provoke her. I brought home a friend and didn't have to worry what she would think. The kitchen and house stayed clean. I slept well. I turned up the radio and danced around and around and around with Emma. I was giddy some afternoons with relief. I felt free.

Here's the plain truth: The four weeks my mother was in the hospital were the best in my life since I had been a young child. Is that a horrible thing to say? It's true. Home was wonderful without my mother. I had fun in school, got to know a girl who is still one of my most treasured friends. I became interested in boys.

Then my mother was diagnosed with schizophrenia, released, and everything slowly went to shit again.

1981

I scan all the psychology books in the library but never check them out—I'm too ashamed. I discover that schizophrenia is bad news. As far as mental illness goes, it's wilderness.

No one knows what causes it. There is no cure. There's no one effective treatment. Some drugs have some effect on some patients. One percent of the world has schizophrenia. That sounds small at first, until I do the math. Is that right? If tens of millions of people have schizophrenia, how come I don't know any other than Mom who has it? Maybe most folks are like me, scared to tell anyone, keeping it to themselves, hunched over a corner table in the public library with all the book spines tucked against the wall. The librarian must think I am reading smutty novels.

The crumbly old psychology books say it is the patient's mother's fault. The new ones say it is something you inherit, though you can't figure it out with a Mendel's box. Some books talk about how to live with a person with schizophrenia at home, which seems to amount to: "Spend all your life caring for your ill family member. But don't forget to take a break every now and then. Get out and see a movie." None of the books satisfy me. None of them even begin to speak to the life we lead at my house. There is no hope to be found in any of these books. Not a tiny bit. I want to quit. I want to rage. I want to find answers. Why does this happen? Why did it happen to us? There must be an answer. And like the child that I was at the cottage, I am back to looking for clues and meaning. I can't stop myself. It's the only hope I have got.

On the way home from the library there is a bag lady, pushing a shopping cart filled with newspapers and talking to herself and laughing. Could my mother wind up that way? Could I?

1981

I believe the doctors are wrong. My mother doesn't need all those pills sent home with her from the hospital in the waxy white bag. The first week back her face twitched and turned until her tongue stuck out and her arms and legs crumpled and my father held her in his arms on the bed crying and holding the phone in his neck until a doctor could be reached to say, "Tardive Dyskinesia. Happens a lot on Prolyxin. We'll switch to Haldol."

"But when does it stop?" my father says into the empty phone. "When will this end?"

My mother says thickly that she does not hear the voices much anymore. She says that it is not the Green Berets speaking to her anymore. She says that she is really psychic. This seems possible to me. She says she does not want to be psychic anymore.

But I know in my heart she is not clairvoyant. I decide that something else is wrong. Something the doctors have never

seen. When I take her supper up to her room at night I close
the door behind me quietly, steadily, until the tongue of the
door clicks in the socket. I wait. Listen to her voice as her
whispers begin again, when she thinks I am gone. I take a
glass scummy with V-8 juice and press its mouth to the wood
and my ear against glass. But nothing she says sounds real.
Most are not even words. At least not words I know. Not
words in this language, at least.

I decide that the doctors are half right. That something is
wrong with her brain, but it is not insanity, not schizophrenia. It's language. Like the boy at school who's dyslexic and
really sees the letters all twisty as if his eyes are a hall of mir-
rors.

So in the morning I get the Jumble out of the paper and
practice breaking the code. There's always a code, from Nancy
Drew to the Rosetta Stone. The trick is finding the key. It's always there, a faint glint in the grass that no matter how hard
you look, when it's found, you're surprised to have stumbled
on it so easily.

I do the Jumble every morning for a week. Then I take my
allowance money and a little from my mother's cracked vinyl
wallet and buy a tape recorder and some cassettes.

When my mother goes to the bathroom, that is when I'll
sneak in. Hide the machine under the bed and leave. Record
my data later.

But it doesn't happen like that. My mother comes back too
soon for me to leave so I am under her bed with the machine.
Her whispers start and I turn the tape on. Her voice is so loud
in the room. And the words she says are words I know, but
jumbled up. So when she laughs, I hadn't realized that some-

thing funny was said. I look at the back of her ankles, all dry and peeling. The soles of her feet are orange and tough. Her toenails are so long they are turning back on themselves, digging. The floor under the bed is thick with dog hair. An open jar of Vicks VapoRub has hardened and lost most of its smell. I try to listen for clues to the code, but my eyes are heavy. There's too much. Even the tape recorder will not be able to fit it all on one side of a cassette. So I stop listening to her words and put my arms across my ears. I wonder how long it will be until she falls dead asleep and I can crawl out from under her and escape.

2000

*D*espite it all, in 1982 when I was fifteen I fell in love. He was tall and lithe, ran cross-country track, made all A's and could rearrange a Rubik's cube so fast that my father was instantly won over by his brilliance. His name was Curry, a family surname turned into his first name. He told me I was beautiful, though most of my friends told me I looked like Kristy McNichol, who I thought was perhaps cute in a boyish way, but never pretty.

When I first brought him home I told him about my mother's schizophrenia soon after we started "going together" and he was kind. He didn't really understand—who could ever understand?—but his acceptance of me and my family made me feel loved.

I was scared of love though. Love felt like something I could never get enough of, and I was always terrified of losing his love. With Curry I felt safe and protected and cherished. I'd loved my mother and she had "betrayed" me by getting ill.

So I knew the stakes. What was frightening and confusing was how my love for him ignited my grief for my mother.

I wept unexpectedly. I believed he would never comprehend why I cried so much, and I, as a teenager, didn't know how to explain my behavior. So instead of saying I really didn't understand why I was so upset all the time, I lied. I made up sad stories for him about other boyfriends I never had, and even went so far as to make up a story about sleeping with an older boy who had treated me badly. That was something that he could comprehend. It was a grief I could understand—even though I had never experienced it. I would tell him these lies, half-believing them myself, and he would hold me and I could weep my wild tears.

Finally, years later, as our relationship deepened, I knew I had to come clean. He was my first boyfriend, my only boyfriend, the only boy I had ever made love with, and I wanted to tell him so. I was terrified he would leave me, that he would stop loving me, but I had to take the chance and let him choose.

When I told him, he was angry. He was hurt. And, unexpectedly, he forgave me.

I think about this now: I was seen at my worst and loved. Forgiven. This still astounds me. And it makes me want to be kinder to people, more compassionate.

I begin to wonder: Can I find a way to forgive my mother for being so sick?

1982

*I*t's Easter. My mother is trying hard to keep things under control. She goes to her psychiatrist. She goes to the Unitarian church with Dad and Emma; she gets up from her afternoon nap to put on her makeup and comb her hair and tries to have dinner ready about the time Dad comes home. We all want her to just stop being sick. For our lives to stop being the constant knot of tension and fatigue and fear. And so we push for wellness. We all try to smile and put forth a huge effort to show one another and the world how normal things are. But for me, it feels like my face will crack from the mask I wear.

Mom and Dad keep on trying, keep on pushing. Mom especially: It's like she's running away from the hospital and her diagnosis as fast as she can. Every day she has filled with activities and little projects like fences she's putting up, so the hospital will never get her or us again. She still talks to herself, but not as much as before, or she's hiding it again. And she's full of energy, she can't stop doing things—on impulse one afternoon she calls and invites her father, stepmother, and my Great-Aunt Bess over for Easter dinner. A family dinner. I don't think we've ever had a family dinner before. She polishes her wedding silver, washes the china that her mother hand-painted when she lived at the YWCA in New York, each dish signed and dated, frets over the Smithfield ham, ruins the pineapple upside-down cake, and then makes another that turns out horribly lopsided. This upsets her. Her mother made perfect pineapple upside-down cake, she keeps saying. She tries to trim the bottom of the cake so it will sit properly and ornaments the top and the cake plate with greenery to conceal the flaw.

My father and mother are in the kitchen together and Emma and I are upstairs, bouncing on my bed and listening to my new Go-Go's album. The California girls sound like they are having big fun and Emma and I pretend we have microphones and are silly boppy California girls in their own girl band. My father tells us to tone it down and we turn off the album and sit on the edge of the bed. It's two hours till my grandfather and his wife and my great-aunt arrive.

I'll braid your hair, I tell Emma and we head downstairs to her room. We hear Mom's voice. She's got that panicky tone, a bit too loud, and the laugh. We all know what the laugh means. It comes in the middle of her sentences, like a cough; it makes my whole body go hard and tight. I stop in the living room, but Emma just heads down the hall, head down, her saddle shoes trudging forward to her room. I feel the mask on my face begin to crack. I am seething. I hate this, I hate her. I wish she would leave. Why doesn't she just leave us, or kill herself? She needs to go.

I walk around the corner. I am going to scream at them to stop. Just quit it, I'll scream. Why don't the two of you just grow up? Shut up? Anything to let her know what she is doing to us. To our family. But right when I get there she is pushing my father out of the kitchen doorway and he bumps into me. O.K., he says, Molly, just calm down. Stop it, just calm down. He tells me to get out of the house. Get Emma and get out of the house. I don't understand what's happening, and then I see that my mother has a large carving knife in her right hand and is pointing it at my father. She is furious, boiling over.

I run, get Emma, and we fly out of the house. Then I am standing still, waiting, stupidly waiting. I don't know what to do. I don't know what to do. Do I call the police?

What will the neighbors think? Will they put her in jail? Oh, God. Why hasn't he come out? Is he cut? Is he hurt? Is he—

"Stay here, Emma Byrd. Don't move." Tears spill out over her face. "Don't cry. C'mon, it'll stop."

"But you're crying," she tells me. She's right. My face is soaked.

I go in the house and it's still going on. My mother has my father cornered in the stairwell. He's crouched down beneath her, his hands up like he's surrendering, but she just keeps going.

"I'm calling the police," I scream. "Stop it, Mom! Stop!"

My father doesn't look away from my mother. "Get the hell out of the house."

"No! I'm calling the police. She's going to kill you."

My mother is laughing and foamy spit is flying out of her mouth. She's like a wild animal.

"I've got it under control. It's under control." My mother lunges at my father and he grabs one wrist. I can't understand what she's talking about. She's just raving.

"No, it's not. I'm going to the Kennedys' and calling the police!"

"Get out, goddammit! Go to the backyard and wait for me."

I go to wait. If he's not out in two minutes I am going to go to the Kennedys' and call the police. But as soon as I reach Emma he is out of the house. Dad is holding the knife and he waves it in the air, to show he's got it.

"Your mom's fine. She just needs to calm down. C'mon, girls. Let's go for a ride." He puts the knife in the glove compartment.

Inside the car my sister cries and I cry and my father cries all the way across the Huguenot Bridge. Then we are cried out. He parks our car in the Pony Pasture lot where the party kids gather in the summer and sun themselves on rocks and drink beer and then smash the bottles when it's time to go home. Today the James River is the color of a nickel. Everything is gray: the sky, the air, the tree branches, the big smooth river rocks. We sit in the car for over half an hour watching the heron and ducks. No one speaks. No one wants to say a word. The quiet inside the car is the best thing in the world to me right now. The next best would be sleep. Just to go away in that quiet and vanish for a while.

My father starts the car. "We need to get back before your grandparents and Bess arrive. Jesus, I hope she's gotten herself together for dinner."

"Do we have to?" Emma asks.

"Yes," my father sighs. "We have to."

We're all quiet again for a minute.

"You girls promise me something," my father says, his voice strangling. "If you've got to get sick, don't get this shit. Get cancer, O.K. At least you die."

1983

I read several passages in library books that say people with schizophrenia aren't violent. But that's not the way things are in my house. And here's something that those psychology books don't mention—most schizophrenics aren't parents. The disease strikes in late adolescence. My mother got it late, after we were born. So she has to deal with her defective brain and with us kids.

I long to understand my mother. I want to know what goes on in her head. So sometimes I mentally restage episodes and try to view them through her eyes, her reality.

At home, I stand in the kitchen and replay a scene from the week before, only now I pretended am my mother.

I combine the profound frustrations that come along with motherhood with severe mental illness. Combine trying to remember to fix supper and clean the house with taking care of a secret war and with managing the transmissions that have started coming in and the other voices in my head that are saying I am nasty I am ugly I am heinous. Along with the fact that I have newly discovered I am psychic along with having a teenager in the house who doesn't listen to a word I say and a psychiatrist who is doping me up with medication that I can barely remember to take.

Combine this with a teenage daughter who is acting snotty and a little girl whining for a peanut butter sandwich. Combine this with a dog that has just shat on the floor and the voice in my head that is now telling me that my husband is having an affair and that my mother knew I would never amount to anything. Combine this with my teenage daughter saying oh-so-snidely that I am full of shit, that I am making all of this up, that if I only *tried* harder I might be able to make my younger daughter her peanut butter sandwich without forgetting the peanut butter, ha ha. Sometimes I mix up my teenage daughter with myself and there's a voice in my head, it's my mother, calling me a tramp, a hussy. But what comes out of my mouth to my teenage daughter is that she is a slut. Look at you. You slut. Look at how you are dressed. Your hem is coming out. I see my daughter's face, contorting, the younger one has slid around the corner with the velvet swish of a cat's tail and the older one is staring back at me, fists clenched by her side. "I hate you," she screams. "I hate you too," I scream back at her, but it is not her that I hate but my own mother, or the idea of her, or the memory of her. But I can't make the voices understand that. They only understand hate. And fight. So when my hand strikes her face and she slaps me right back I grab her hand, I'm still stronger, and then her hair, and then I drag her down the hall and through her bedroom. I think she is screaming. You will not do this to me, I hear my voice rage at her. You will not treat me this way. My daughter kicks me and gets away. Leaves, goes to work at Sears in the mall. Her hem coming out. Later, I will call and apologize. But there is no forgiveness, no under-standing. Only this, day in, day out: This unraveling; this fight; this incredible drag.

1983

The winter before I leave for college, I write a term paper on Virginia Woolf. I am a C and D student, but I have discovered literature and writing. I read Quentin Bell's biography of Woolf. Reading about Woolf's illness makes me softer toward my mother. I've pushed her away too much. I read her a poem I have written. Knowing that I am leaving relaxes me some. I'm going to get out. I'm going to have a life. She looks at me and says, "It's so sad." I clip it back in my binder.

I tell my mother that Virginia Woolf heard voices too and my mother is fascinated.

Really?

Yes, she thought the birds were speaking to her. But she struggled and wrote many books.

She's very beautiful, my mother says, flipping through Woolf's early photos. Look at those eyes. Oh, she gasps, when she sees later pictures where the circles under her eyes are

deep and her face plainly reveals its sorrow. Oh, she looks awful. Whatever happened to her?

I'm shocked by a sudden urge to protect my mother from
the truth. And then flooded with an awesome guilt. How
could I have ever wanted my mother dead? I was so upset
when I read accounts of Woolf's drowning herself. It seemed
a horrible way to die. I imagined that she had a change of
heart, and then couldn't free the stones she had placed in her
pockets. That she struggled against herself then too, but was
swept away.

"She hiked a lot," I tell my mother. "And wrote letters, lots
of letters to friends. It was hard. But she hung in there."

Mom nods and pats my knee. "That's good."

"I need to get back to work," I tell her and she rises from
the edge of my bed to leave.

"This is nice," she says, wanting to linger, but I can't give in
now. I refuse to raise my head from my book until I hear the
floor creak and know that she has gone.

1984

*T*he night before I am to leave my mo-
ther's house for college I am violently ill and awake vomiting.
Sheer nerves. It occurs to me that I've almost never been away
from my mother. I once spent three days with my cousins, but
that's it. I have never been to camp. Never been on my own.

Since I have almost failed out of high school my first year
away is in one of those places that is more boot camp for re-
medial students than college. After a year I bring up my
grades and transfer to a good school back in Fairfield and rent
an apartment with an old high-school classmate. I hang in
there, I work hard, but I am a wreck almost every day, my
stomach torn to shreds, my nails bitten down so far my fingertips burn.

I am a misfit, I think. I am stupid. It doesn't even occur to
me that the fact I am so terrified and miserable every day is remotely connected to my mother and my life when I was at
home with her. Then one of my professors asks about my

home life and I briefly mention my mother's illness like it's where she's employed. "Oh," she says not unkindly. "That explains the old woman in you." Oddly, for the first time, I am deeply relieved to tell someone about my mother and to have them tell me that they have noticed something was wrong. Yes, I think. My father, my sister, me—we are marked. The few people I choose as friends are those like my professor, who refuse to look away.

1986

I visit home every week and check on Emma and my father. I'm a junior in college, she is making into adolescence—right on schedule she is growing up and growing remote. My mother is off her medication, refuses to go back on it, and there is nothing anyone can do. She prowls the house, raving and screaming. My father has moved down to the den to sleep and has become listless and depressed. I beg him to leave my mother. I worry about Emma. But he doesn't know what to do. He's so used to being stuck he can't seem to move now. It's horrible to see him this way, frozen by his pain.

Curry is at college four hours away and we see each other every four or six weeks. So I talk my father into going out on Friday nights with me when Emma is sleeping over at a friend's. We go to a movie or supper and he has a beer or two or a glass of wine and seems to loosen up. We talk about Mom and what he could do. You could rent an apartment, I tell him. They're not too expensive. Something close to the high school. And he thinks on this. He has done everything he can legally do, I reassure him. Everything anybody will let him do to help my mother. Now he has to help Emma and himself.

It's February of my junior year in college when my father's father dies. They have been mildly estranged for many years. I am sad for my father's loss, but I really didn't know my grandfather. The funeral is out of state and Dad asks me if I will check in on Emma every day when he is gone.

On the day my father is to return I go to the house. Mom is upstairs with the stereo going full blast the way she does when the voices in her head get going. I can hear her footfalls overhead and her muttering and laughter. I go to check on my sister. Emma is in her closet, reading, the way she likes to do. She has devised a system so that my mother can't bother her. She wrenches off the hollow doorknob to her room and locks the door from the inside, then she does the same to her closet door. There, in her room in a room, she feels safe.

I knock and she lets me in. "Hey, it's WMOM today," I say. Mom's got the radio going so loud you can feel the beat throughout the house.

"Yeah," says Emma in her best FM radio deejay voice— "WMOM—all crazy, all the time."

We sit in her closet and talk for a while. She is so sad and I hate to think of her in the house without me. Yet I am so glad not to be living in that house. Emma and I make a snack in the kitchen and I pick up the phone to make a call. My mother comes downstairs. She looks terrible. She's got on a pair of too-tight corduroys held together at the waist by a kilt pin, a filthy pink sweater, and she smells foul. "Get off the phone, Gingie, it's tapped."

"Here we go again," I say to my sister. My mother reaches for the receiver. "Buzz off," I tell her and keep dialing.

She grabs the receiver from my hand and I snatch it back, then she wrenches the receiver from my hand and slams it into my face. I am stunned and fall back against the counter. My mouth and cheek are sour with blood. I cross my arms across my face and the receiver strikes my arms again and again. I see Emma's shirt leave the room and hear her door slam. I scream after her. "Get out of the house and get in my car. Go." I walk into the living room so Mom can't get Emma and I hear her run down the hall toward the kitchen. "Lock the car doors!" I holler.

In the living room my mother slaps me and grabs my hair. Normally, if you can call occasions such as this normal, I fight to get out, but today, something in me is enraged, furious beyond all imagining. I fight to win. I knock her to the floor and get in a few good cuffs of my own. She's crying. Fuck her. Let her cry. I have had it. I feel good having knocked her down after all the times that she has hurt me. I wish I could kill her. If I had a gun in my hand, I might. I really might. And I am glad I don't have a gun, because I don't want to know what I am capable of. I get up to leave. She screams and follows behind me but only up to the doorway. For some reason she refuses to cross that threshold.

In my car Emma and I sit and cry. "It's going to be O.K.," I tell her and myself, over and over, until my shakes subside. Then I realize that I have left my car keys in the house. When I go back inside to get them Mom is on me again and I have to elbow her away. She stands behind me and screams words at me like one long wail. I get my keys and leave.

Once we're at my apartment Emma and I get ourselves calmed down. She curls up in my room and I fix her some soup. I call a friend from college to drive me to the airport since I am so shakes. I want to meet my father's flight that evening before he gets home and Emma calls a friend on the phone to talk and cry. I think perhaps I should call the police, but I know from talking to the counselors at college that the best I can hope for is that they will take my mother away for a three-day evaluation: They will drug her, she will appear before a judge, appear sane enough, and come home with meds that she will refuse to take and real attitude to boot. To get her to stay longer, she'd have to sign herself in. And that isn't going to happen. I decide against calling. We have never called when we needed to: Maybe if we did, then she would have a history and she could get help and we could get out. But we are too humiliated and frightened and stunned when my mother gets violent.

At the airport that night I am scared. Scared that my father will not believe me. Scared that he will be mad at me. These are not rational fears; they are the fears of a child, or someone who has just been beaten up, but I am scared nonetheless. People in the airport look at me with my scratched face, swollen lip and cheek, and then look at my friend, a six-foot-four hulk of a fellow. What must they think?

When my father comes down the jetway he looks so tired. And he's surprised to see me. Then he looks at my face, asks what happened, and I recount the story in one hot rush of words. He shakes the hand of my friend and sends him home.

Then my father hugs me tight and I cry. In his car the whole way back to my apartment, I tell him that he has to leave. He has to get out. He's got to do something. For Emma. They cannot go on living like this. Mom's not bad, she's sick, but he cannot sacrifice Emma to this. He cannot sacrifice himself to this. We should be able to get Mom hospitalized, and maybe we can for a bit, but then it's a few weeks in and she stops taking her medication. She goes delusional again. You can't wait until she tries to kill us or kill herself. That may never happen. I am covered in tears, my father's face is soaked. Neither of us bother to wipe them away.

Dad looks worn out and frozen. He's lived so many years with this that I don't think he can even imagine a life without the daily dread of my mother. But I will not stop pushing him. He tells me that's enough, he's heard me, he's had a hard week, he understands the situation, but I don't stop, I come at him with the same intensity that I used to fight my mother. It's time. I'm determined to do whatever it takes to get him to leave.

Three weeks later he rents an apartment. Dad and Emma and I move in together. The apartment won't take dogs and Ralph, who has been incontinent for the past two years and whom my father has cared for and cleaned up after because he has been unable to face the thought that this poor dog is at the end of his days, must be put down.

My mother is left alone in the house, psychotic, unable to care for herself yet still legally beyond psychiatric help. But we know that moving out is the only way he can save Emma, my mother, and himself.

We bring my mother groceries every week and my father

checks in on her daily. It is excruciatingly sad, but still, we are the happiest we have ever been. My sister's grades improve, my father begins to date a wonderful woman, and I apply for graduate schools. We can sleep at night. When we leave the apartment in the morning we do not dread what we will face when we come home. Slowly we begin to relax, just a bit, and begin to see a future that includes caring for my mother, but not one that involves being ruled each minute of our lives by her illness.

1987

*H*i, Mrs. Roberts, how are you today? It's the social worker. We've called her out to take a look at the conditions my mother is living in. To see how delusional she is. She needs help. This visit is merely a formality to be got through. Once the social worker talks to my mother and sees how ill she is, we will sigh with satisfaction and relief. At last someone will understand the enormity of the situation, then something can and will be done. The home evaluation is an unfortunate, yet necessary, humiliation.

My father and the social worker meet at the house. She gets out of a white state-issued car. My father is in his business suit, taking an early lunch from the bank. He is thin and handsome and affable, his skin has crinkled flatteringly about his eyes, a sparkly blue. You could mistake these creases for laugh lines, true laugh lines, but I can't recall the last time I really saw my father laugh when it wasn't tinged with pain or bitterness or simply faked for the benefit of others. But the social worker doesn't see this of course and there's no way to explain that to her, that the gentle kind concerned man she sees before her is beaten raw inside. That he hasn't laughed or loved in years. In the eyes of the law these things do not matter. His sacrifices to my mother and her illness do not matter. The fact that he gets up and goes to work every day and pays the bills and forces himself to run and take care of himself and get his daughters ready for school every day simply does not matter.

What matters is that the house we lived in together and where my mother now lives alone is in a good neighborhood. A better neighborhood than the social worker's, no doubt. What matters is that when the social worker says how are you today, Mrs. Roberts, that my mother responds, I'm fine. That when the social worker asks if she is feeling well, my mother says brightly, "I'm feeling just fine." That when the social worker says, "What year is it, Mrs. Roberts," that she says it is 1987. She thinks Carter may be President, but she can't really recall, isn't that interested in politics, and the social worker nods in agreement. "Do you want to hurt yourself, Mrs. Roberts?" "Oh no." "Are you thinking of hurting anybody else?" "Of course not!" she says indignantly.

Should we lie? Exaggerate? It would be for her benefit. No, it would be for ours. Robertses don't lie, my father says, echoing his father's words. Robertses let the experts do their job. Surely, she will see the truth.

She looks around the house. It's dirty all right. The floors are sticky, the carpet matted with coffee spills and cat urine. The windows are cobwebbed and blurred with grime. The sills are scattered with fly husks. Mom's begun a collection of two-liter Coke bottles in the utility room. But you cannot be locked up for being a slob. In fact, it will take a lot more than this to even get her involuntarily evaluated by a psychiatrist.

Dad and the social worker stand on the front porch. "She seems competent," the social worker says, and begins the paperwork.

"She's very sick. She's delusional." My father pleads with her as they sign forms.

"You can't just be delusional. Your wife is not a danger to herself or anybody else."

"But she leaves the burners on. I have to bring her food. She won't leave, she talks to herself and paces day and night. She's insane and doesn't think she's insane. She won't take her medicine."

"But she's not a danger to herself or anyone else."

"Are you kidding? She can't care for herself. If I didn't bring her food she wouldn't eat."

"Now, if she wasn't eating, then that we could classify as a danger to herself."

Silence. An opportunity.

"No. I can't do that. *That's* insane."

Shrug. Palms turned upward. "Your wife has rights under the law."

"What else? What counts as a danger to oneself or others? What? Tell me."

The social worker pauses. "I'm sorry. The way the law reads, Mr. Roberts, unless she's cut herself or somebody else, there's not much can be done."

1989

*W*hat my father saw.

The February night is fourteen degrees and my father is making his twice weekly visit to my mother's house to bring her groceries and to check in on her. He's tried for two years to get her involuntarily committed. She refuses to leave the house and cannot take care of herself: burners are left on, she won't bathe for days, and she raves at all hours of the day and night. Yet the laws are on her side and she is allowed to remain untreated because she is not seen as a danger to herself or others.

That night my father walks into the house and it is dark. No lights will come on. Everything is still and cold. My father swallows hard. He finds my mother in the backroom huddled under piles of clothes. When he asks what has happened to the heat, she tells him she has taken care of the wiretaps. He gets a flashlight from the utility room and sees live wires from the furnace on the concrete floor. He scans the house, finding plaster dust and exposed beams in the walls where my mother has tried to remove every electrical outlet. He is nauseated and relieved. Surely, he thinks, this is bad enough to get her help. Surely this can be defined as a danger to oneself. When he calls, the social workers grudgingly agree to commit her and send two men from the sheriff's department to handcuff my mother, so ill, and take her away. My father stands on the porch and watches as neighbors who haven't spoken to us in years spill out onto their porches to watch as my mother is taken away.

She could have electrocuted herself, he later told my sister and me. We bit our lips against the unspeakable thought: It might have been easier on everyone if she had just died.

Right then my father's paradox becomes clear—he understands my mother is truly ill, but he also believes that the woman he had loved still has the potential to resurrect herself. My sister and I will learn compassion slowly and through the back door—our rage at the lives we lived during our childhood turning slowly to grief, then compassion, then kindness, then finally love—a sort of Kübler-Ross inversion that will take years to complete.

1989

I'm out. I live in North Carolina, a whole state away, and I am in graduate school. My boyfriend and I live together. But I am haunted by my mother and my grief. I wake up nights from my dead dreamless sleep tears all over my face, sobbing, lean over for my boyfriend and then cry myself back to sleep in the tight cradle of his arms and legs and chest. He murmurs, he holds on, this is all he can do and it is all that I want him to do. I wake up the next day with my guts sore from crying, the muscles in my back and chest spasm throughout the day from the nearly nightly workout I give them.

Finally, I agree to see a therapist. I hate going to the shrink's, but I know I need to. I don't go to the shrink's for answers, only out of desperation. She is bound to know some way of fixing this. The sobs are grief, I am smart enough to know that, I don't need someone to diagnose why I am crying, that's plain to see: I feel safe enough to cry now. O.K. But I don't know how to live with this pain and dread, which has stalked me since I left home. I am on guard all the time, in exactly the same way I was at home with Mom. Waiting for the next bad thing to happen. When I was in a room with her I stayed near the doorways. When I was in the house with her, I tried to keep the two key deadbolts unlocked. It was easier to run out if I didn't have to fumble with a key. When she started to gear up I hid the wine or poured inches out of the bottle so she would run out—crazy was bad, drunk and crazy were worse.

I never did manage it well. And there was always a next time. So then I lived against her. Lived to get out. So why this dread and agony? Why now? I'm out; I made it; I'm free. Except I am not. There's a beast with its claws in me like deep hooks. And it's growing off me, its claws winding through every inch of who I am. Why do I see the shrink? Simple. I need a plan. I need to know how to kill this beast.

In the parking lot outside her office I am overcome with nerves so bad I can smell the rapid sweat from the soles of my feet, my pits, and my pubes. I sit in the car, windows rolled up and count the three minutes I have left before I will be late. I get out of the car when I have thirty seconds left. I walk into the building, twenty-seven steps to the door. Eight to the elevator, which no one seems to use, since the door springs open as soon as I press the button. Two floors up, then out and straight ahead to the waiting room with its ancient magazines and worn carpet. My shrink shows up and nods once at me (she borrows the office from another friend who's a shrink), rattles through her keys to get in, and then clicks the door behind her.

"So," she says, once we're both seated. I look at her face. It's kind. Also rebuilt. She has a faint web of scarring that her heavy makeup can't hide. Smashed perhaps by windshield or rocks. I feel slightly sorry for her and figure this is her reason for being a therapist.

The feeling hits—I'm panicked, there's a wall of water headed toward me. I can't take it here. I have to get out. This woman can't help me. I can't tell her anything. I am miserable. I am wretched. I couldn't tell her why I have come to see her if my life depended on it. And my life does depend upon it. The first couple of sessions I told her about my mother, her schizophrenia, her history. Now there's nothing left to say.

"This isn't working. I just don't know how to do this." I look away, focus on the desk leg.

"How does that make you feel?"

"What?"

She twists around in her chair to catch my gaze.

"Feel. How does that make you feel?"

"How does what make me feel?"

"What you just said."

My mind's gone blank from fear. "Uh. What did I just say?"

She rolls her eyes at me.

"You said that you don't know how to do this." She touches her hair right above her scars. "And I asked how that makes you feel."

"Oh." I feel my mouth grimace. "I don't know."

Silence.

"I mean, I guess I mean, how do I do this?"

"What?" She squints, scrapes her pencil loudly across the

yellow pad in her lap, and flips the page. The sound makes me want to tear off my ears.

"This," I say and wave my hand. "Therapy."

"How do you want to do this? It's your hour."

"I don't think this is going to work. It's not helping. I don't know how to do this. It's too expensive. I'm a grad student. I make eight-thousand dollars a year and you charge eighty an hour. And I don't feel any better."

"You want to feel better?"

"Yes!" Now we're getting somewhere.

"But that's not the goal of therapy. It's not supposed to make you feel better. It's supposed to help you understand yourself. Self-knowledge is the goal here."

"But knowing yourself helps you feel better, right?"

"No, the truth doesn't make you happier."

"But I want to feel better too."

Silence.

"This isn't working. I don't know how to do this. I think I should stop seeing you."

"So leave," she says.

1989

I made a desperate pact with myself. It went like this: I can make a life for myself. But I will not marry or have a child. I can fall in love, but I cannot wind up a wife and mother, because that is what my mother did. It must be what drove her mad. That seems to be the general conclusion I am to draw after almost a decade of literature courses. Crazy women are domesticated beasts turned feral. And my mother did seem to get worse after the birth of children, so maybe hormones were it. I can't take the pill—she couldn't take the pill. Yes, it was definitely tied into the hormones. So no kids. And no marriage. Nothing at all that could even remotely make me like my mother. Nothing at all.

But then I got married. But the deal was—no kids. Years after that, I had a child. So I revised. Simply, no getting sick. Sick meaning crazy. If I think I am getting as sick as my mother, then I have a moral responsibility not to subject my family and child to the same wretchedness that I endured. No one

227

can live like that. I could not, would not, do that to those I loved. I would never do that to my child. It would be unacceptable. So that was the deal. Too ill, then death. I thought it was rational. Positively responsible. Noble even. Yes, it was noble. Japanese. The child would never understand the sacrifice. Would grieve for what he perceived as potential lost, perhaps even hate me, but at least he would never know the pain of existence in a house with a madwoman. Yes. This was the bargain I made with myself.

This was how I lived my life.

1990

*C*urry and I decide to wed. My mother is too ill to invite, and leaving her out is easier on everyone. Yet my longing for my mother—my mother healthy, my fantasy mother—is everywhere. It's in the dressing room of the thrift store where I find my wedding dress and where Curry, not my mother, buttons the seventy-five fragile silk-covered buttons up my back. It's in the front row at our ceremony, where she doesn't sit crying as I leave our family to form another.

I realize that my mother's absence is how I've defined myself. Suddenly I think of Patty Hearst again. Citizen Tania could never have existed without the erasure of Patty. But what about when it was all over and Tania wanted to be Patty again? How did Tania ever manage to rescue Patty Hearst? I imagine that Patty hated her history the same way I hate mine. And that she wondered too: After such a life, how will I ever manage to become myself?

After our wedding I inherit a box of photos from my

mother's family. I try to chronologically order the pictures of my mother. I study her eyes. When she was a baby she looks happy, but then, around six or seven, her eyes look distant and she is clearly unhappy. Is this a clue? Was there something that happened in my mother's childhood that made her the way she is? If I can figure this out, will it help her? Even if it doesn't, if what is wrong with her isn't schizophrenia, won't that mean that I won't get it? And that if I have children they won't be at risk? Won't it mean that I can stop asking Curry, "Did you hear that?" when I hear a faint voice in the distance?

2000

I set out to get answers. After all, I am writing a book. "Tell me about Mom's first hospitalization. I don't remember her leaving, I just remember her being gone." My father sighs. "Oh, God. I don't know how I ever managed to talk her into seeing a psychiatrist that led to her first hospitalization. I somehow got her to see Dr. Howard to prove to me that I was wrong and that she was really just fine. If he tells me I'm wrong, then I will believe it, was what I told her. And she wanted me to shut up and to be proven right, so she went. He interviewed her and then she agreed to let him admit her to MCV. I don't know how he did it."

We both get choked up on the phone for a minute and can't speak. "I just want it to go away," I wail.

"What?"

"It still makes me so sad. I want to stop being sad."

"You're not always sad," Dad says, and I feel hot tears begin to stream down my face.

"You have to realize that in a way she is dead. I sort of think of Mom as an old relative in a nursing home. I care, but there's not much I can do. I have to go on. It doesn't do any good to spend your whole life mourning. It's not going to save her and it hurts you and the people who love you.

"You know," he says "it will be good when you're done with this book. It's not good to spend your days in the past. I hope when you are finished that you'll find something that's more fulfilling."

But right now I cannot even think of being fulfilled. I am compelled still. Searching for clues and meaning in every word my father speaks, and in every silence. I look for reasons the same way I did as a child. I just want to find some way to make sense of this. Then I can move on. But right now I am stuck, wanting either to resurrect my mother to health or bury her. I feel crushed, literally, these days, as if the bones in my body are broken from both the weight of her presence and her absence.

So when I get a letter from my mother that corresponds almost exactly to a childhood nightmare of mine, I think I have finally hit gold. A connection.

The Dream

The first dream I ever recall having is set in the cottage. I was three or four years old. I do not know if I had the dream while my family was visiting our cottage in Kechotan on one of our many summer weekend visits. In the dream, I am in the bathroom, the only room in the cottage where the walls extend all the way up to the roof. The only private room in the house. The rest of the house is dark; everyone is sleeping. Perhaps I have gotten up to pee. I pull myself up and into the cracked and graying bowl of the sink so that I can see my face in the mirror. I press my hands hard against the cool glass. Beside me the wall groans open, sliding back into itself like a pocket door. Inside the wall, almost flat against it, are a group of people who are not people. Everyone is costumed. As an adult, when I see my first Hieronymus Bosch painting, I will think of this dream. One tall dream man is a skeleton. There is a nap to his costume, like fake fur. When I pass by him the black background of his costume smudges onto me like the dust from a dark moth's wing. I am horrified. Two other costumed people have red-and-yellow-striped drinking straws in their mouths and they use them to blow pills down my throat. I remember the space inside the walls as being narrow and tight. I remember thinking that I always knew there were people in between the walls. Then, in dream magic, I am standing in the bathroom again. I bang the heel of my hands on the mirror. I press the walls with my hands and ears. Suddenly I doubt everything I have seen. I want to see that wall roll back a second time.

THE LETTER

My thirty-third Birthday
Durham, N.C.
The James Madison Home, Fairfield, Virginia

Dear Gingie,

Happy Birthday a few days—left—late. I love you and hope your day was wonderful. I just wish I could be with you all.

I heard about the new car. I know the three of you are really excited about it. V.W. makes a fine car in my opinion.

I've got a terrible cold and I am disturbing my roommate by snorting. I must be really a mess in my sleep.

I am having a time from hearing you, Emma and Tom under this place and I don't know what to do for it. I don't know what to do about it. It's not just you all, there are kids under this house screaming Mom.

Dad and Dr. Chatterjee are putting me in another place. This place is about to lose their license because it doesn't pass the state inspection. I don't know if it is going to be any better but I hope not.

I live scared around these people and I think they are going to do harm to me.

It seems I have lived here before and Pat Webb drugged me when we lived in Kensington years ago. It must have been twenty years ago. Oh, Gingie, try to understand. Gingie, I'm not crazy there are people in the walls making noise. I don't know what to say so it continues and also gas in the walls.

I know it's moonshine and children in the walls.

Maybe when you come sometime you can hear it. Kids naked screaming their lungs out—calling Mom, Mom, Mom.

Maybe they won't have at the new place. I'm afraid to talk and Dad just—shrugs—ignores it and goes on. Hon—I've got to go to bed now. I'll send this letter with Dad tomorrow.

You be very careful because they could steal these children.

I give my love to you three.

Love,
Mom

P.S. Take care

I am back to looking for clues. A way to unlock the past and to somehow rescue my mother. Or, if not that, at least a way to understand my past in a meaningful, clear, lucid way. The walls.

I know that there is nothing in those walls for me, but what I cannot shake is the urge to go to the cottage and open up the bathroom wall. Just to see. Just to make sure there's nothing in there I need to know about.

The place keeps pulling at me.

2000

*M*y husband, son, and I drive to Kecho-tan from Fairfield, an hour away. It takes me a while to figure out how to find our way there, there's not a good sign from the highway, and we wind up in Newport News asking for directions at two different places before someone recognizes the name of the town. It's only fifteen miles away, for God's sake, but you'd think we were looking for the Lost Colony the way people squint when we ask if we're on the right road.

Finally we approach the small bridge on the edge of town. and there's the giant space monster, the name my cousins and I gave the red-and-white steel structure five stories high and an acre across, that's still stands in the field near Langley.

"What's that?" Thomas asks. I tell my son the story of the astronauts who used to train here, but then were called away to Florida, along with all the jobs and NASA money. The monster was built for them to use as some sort of training.

"What's it used for now?"

"Not a goddamned thing. It just sits there, like a pyramid."

My husband gives me an elbow. "Your mouth," he scolds. I have a bad habit of cussing when I'm nervous.

Before we go to the cottage I stop beside the woods. The trees are gone and the land is all torn up and stumpy. Raped is the only word that comes to mind. This used to be a lush place, always green. Now it's sand and dead wood. Bright pink plastic ribbons flutter on stakes to mark the new owner's boundaries. I walk over to my great grandfather's grave, which is undisturbed, but weirdly exposed.

My son walks down toward the shore. The water is tense and distant beyond us, stretched tight as a highwire. It's a low sky day; it will storm tonight. My husband is on the edge of the property, shaking hands with an elderly man. I walk over and tell him I used to live here. He knows my people and yet all the time we lived here, I never spoke to this man. It's typical of old Kechotan. Not unfriendliness, just a type of clannish propriety that kept everyone separate. His brother owned the wooded plot and has sold it to an orthopedic surgeon in Yorktown for his summer house. He assures me that there are provisions for the grave. Won't be disturbed, family can come visit and tend to the grave.

I nod.

The old man looks at the ruined ground. "Makes me sick."

"Yes. It used to be such a pretty place. I played back here as a girl."

"I mean the graves. My brother didn't tell the owner about the other graves."

"The children," I say, and I suddenly remember the stones worn smooth, the dates gone but a little lamb still visible.

"It's just wrong," he says, and jams his hands into his pockets. "Headstones were washed away long ago in some another flood or storm, but they're here. Someone ought to get a pole and tap around."

I think about this for a second, but then realize that anything in this earth, even bones and coffin lids, would be nothing but soil now. We're just both mad to see our history being bought by foreigners, the name given to anyone whose family doesn't go back over five generations.

I nod. "Well, thanks. I'm gonna look around a bit and then go over to our property."

"Welp, nice to meet you," he tells me and leaves.

*   *   *

Our driveway isn't visible anymore except for the crepe myrtle trees my mother and father planted over twenty years ago to mark its path. My husband and I drive up as far as we can and then walk the rest of the distance, through the tangle of grapevines and tickweed that covers the drive's entrance to our woods. Mayflies are all over us and Thomas screams until he's sprayed head to toe with Off.

Our land is so beautiful. Not overgrown, mostly old pine trees and a soft spongy floor. It's the sort of forest you imagine Daniel Boone saw one morning and decided he'd take a nice, long walk. In my mind this is such a sad place but now that I am here I am awed by the beauty of this land. I find it almost impossible to believe that anything so awful could happen here. Then I wonder how much the land sheltered and saved me and my sister.

I walk up to the cottage. Part of the roof has torn like fabric and hangs inside the house. I'm going to look inside, I tell my son. Do you want to come?

He sticks his face up to the hole in the door. "Ew. No way. Dad said we can go look at the cove." My husband kisses me. I watch as he and Thomas walk toward the cove. I step inside and hear things retreat to the corners, bugs and mice. This is more their home than mine. The stovepipe rattles in the wind.

For a house we abandoned, there is still so much of us left behind. There's the refrigerator, decoupaged like some sort of outsider art. There's a Ziggy picture on the wall above the sink that reads It's better to look where you're going, than where you've been—especially if you're not too crazy about where you've been. The sign above the front door that points to our rafters reads Psychiatrist, One Floor Up. They are perversely humorous and retroactively portentous. Some weird joke placed in this corrupted time capsule.

It's cold in here. My shoes scratch in the leaves and trash on the floor. Am I nuts? I say aloud. But I am here with a purpose.

I go straight to the bathroom. I turn the flashlight on and set it on the shelf beside me. There's more light in this room than there's been in twenty-five years. God, look at it. It's filthy—dust and dirt and God knows what other nastiness layered thick on the shelves. There's a black bristled curler of my mother's. There's an orange box of foot powders and an ancient bar of soap, cracked and stained with mold. There's a conch shell filled with cigarette butts. A curling iron and electrical cord that's turned brittle and powdery. Is anything here worth claiming?

I kneel down and place my hand flat against the place on the wall where I will strike with my hammer. Why this spot exactly? What's here? I press my hand and cheek against this spot as if I am hoping to sense movement behind it or warmth. Do I expect to hear the drub of a heartbeat?

It surprises me how the hammer bounces off the wall. And how loud the collison rings out. I decide I don't care, I swing the thing hard, two-handed swings. Slowly I begin to make dents in the wall. If the walls here were plaster or drywall, I'd already be through, but these are hard old wooden walls. I slam the hammer into the wall again and again and the cabinet doors above me fly open and shudder. Bottles tremble against each other and then leap from the cabinet and land on my head or the floor. Let them. I want to go wild, to swing this hammer until the whole place falls down; until I fall apart with it. I close my eyes and pound. I can't breathe. The air is thick with dust and filth and my eyes burn. I cover my mouth and nose with my turtleneck. I'm sweating from my efforts and still the wall yields nothing more than a few dents. I try the clawed side, but I can't even manage the tiniest hole.

I sit on the commode and look at the wall and the half-moon dents and scratches I have made. I may have to get my husband in here, he's stronger. No. I have to do this myself. But it could take me an hour or more. Then I hear my son and husband as they walk back from the cove, their voices growing clearer. "Daddy, look!" I heard him squeal. Then wild delighted laughter. "I want to show Mom!"

"You need to wait." My husband told him.

Should I stay in this dark filthy room and pound away at a wall while they wait for me outside? What's wrong with me?

My life isn't here—it's right outside. Waiting for me. Waiting to show me something. There's nothing here for me in this house, this room, this wall. The girl I was when we lived here is gone. But I am here, grown. Should I remain captive to my past? Someone once told me that people were like water: the shapes we took dependant on all the outside forces. We could turn into snowflakes or ice, puddles or steam and back again. We were malleable, our personalities, our identities fluid.

I hated the analogy when I heard it and I hated it even more now as I remembered it. I was no passive drop of water. Bullshit, I thought. I got to choose. And I was choosing—to leave.

I gathered my things and looked in the mirror. I was gray as a ghost, my hair was full of filth. My eyebrows and eyelashes too. I looked as if I were covered in chalk. I brushed some of it off, but it made me gag. Should I smash in the mirror as one final dramatic gesture? No. Nothing I could destroy would remedy this grief for this place, for the time we lived here, for my mother and her ruined life.

I'd like to say I found something here. I'd like to say I left some sort of talisman behind. Some sweet farewell. But I simply walked out. Whatever I lost here was truly lost. I'd come hoping to unlock some strong emotion, to have some sort of cathartic event, but what I found here was cold and long dead. It was just a sad old house, falling in and neglected. Almost ordinary.

Thomas runs up to me. "Mama, look at this!" He opens his cupped hand to reveal a fiddler crab, waving one giant claw in the air, his small pincer held tight to his body.

"He'll pinch my thumb. Watch!"

"That doesn't hurt?"

"A little. Isn't he cool? There lots of them in the mud. But this one was just walking on the pier."

"He's beautiful." His giant claw white and blue and orange. Spidery legs. Eyes glossy as fish eggs.

I watch Thomas study the crab and marvel at my son. Age six and willing to withstand the pinch of a crab in order to see it up close.

My husband dusts off my shoulders and my hair.

"You O.K.?"

I nod. "I couldn't get through. The walls are wood." And I don't care anymore.

"We'll have to bring a crowbar next time," he says.

"No." I'm firm. "There's no next time."

"Can I keep the fiddler crab? I'll put him in the aquarium. Please. He's so cute!"

"No, sweetie. He lives here. Go put him back where you found him. It's time for us to go home."

2000

*T*hree weeks later we visit my mother. My son tries to be patient. He understands that grandma's brain is broken, and that some of the people in this home are a bit like children—they can't take care of themselves without help. We walk outside to the garden. My son throws a tennis ball with the resident Labrador retriever while I visit with Mom.

I ask about her health and she starts in on an unexpected delusional riff. "You know Dr. Chaterjee has a picture of you when you were a baby. It's on his desk. You're wearing red tights and you are sitting in a big china bowl just as happy as you can be. Dr. Chaterjee is mad with your father for dating his secretary, because Dr. Chaterjee wants her all to himself. She's a real hottie pants. Do you remember that picture? You are just the cutest thing."

I never know what to do when she is like this. Sometimes I just let her go. Others I get mad at her and we fight. Mostly I just try to change the topic and cut the visit short, convinced that my presence is somehow stressing her out and that I am responsible for activating her psychosis. But this time I just take a breath and make up my mind that if I am to have any dealing with my mother that will be meaningful to me I can't ignore it. I can't pretend to buy into it. I can't try to tease the truth from it. I have to speak honestly.

"No," I tell her, and I hear my voice tremble a bit as I try to speak calmly. "You're wrong." My mother looks at me, hurt and confused. "Your doctor doesn't have a picture of me. Dad is not in love with his secretary. What you are saying isn't real."

I know that my mother believes what she is saying is true, and I fear that I am being cruel by leveling with her.

"No, Gingie," she insists, "the picture of you—"

"It's a delusion. I'm sure Dr. Chaterjee has a picture of his children, but he doesn't have one of me." My mother appears shaken for a minute. Then, she sighs and says, sadly, and from some still sane part of herself, "Oh. Well, maybe that's just how I wanted it to be."

Her remark strikes me harder than a physical blow to my head. A fierce centralized pain, then spangles like a star exploding, then dark numbness. Then, slowly, my feeling returns and brings with it a sudden opening like a night-blooming flower unfurling its petals inside me. Right then, I am overcome with love and relief.

Yes, I think. There have been so many wishes.

But this—my mother sitting in front of the goldfish pond, me sitting beside her, our arms linked for this moment—this is how it is.

Acknowledgments

Many friends and colleagues have helped me over the years and their mere mention here cannot begin to express my gratitude: Sheri Holman, Frances Dowell, Nancy Richard, Marjorie Hudson, David Rowell, Dawn Raffel, Nancy Peacock, Albert La Farge, Brendan O'Malley, Jane Snyder, Phil Spiro, Anastasia Toufexis, Doris Iarovici, Mirinda Kossoff, Cynthia Cannell, Denise Roy, Nancy Fann, Tara Parsons, Annie Dillard, and Joanne Greenberg.

Special thanks to the Virginia Center for the Creative Arts and the Durham, North Carolina, Arts Council for their support during the writing of this book.